Moving Mountains

Keys to Prayer That Works!

Laurie Blank

Copyright © 2014 Laurie Blank
All rights reserved.

ISBN: 1461106788
ISBN-13: 9781461106784
Library of Congress Control Number: 2011906262
CreateSpace Independent Publishing Platform
North Charleston, South Carolina

All scripture quotes are in *Italics and are* taken from NKJV, KJV, NIV or AMP Bible, with emphasis added.

This book is dedicated to:

My Lord, Savior, and love of my life, Jesus Christ. To Him goes all the glory for the words in this book.

My husband: Thank you - for our marriage, for our family, and for standing with me through thick and thin. I love you, with all of my heart.

My children: Words cannot describe my love for you. The Lord's great love for me, and for humankind as a whole, is demonstrated to me in that He blessed me with four of the most wonderful children on Earth. I thank Him for you daily and I thank you, for being my babies.

My readers: This book was written out of a love for the people on this earth and a deep desire to share the great love of Jesus with you. Know that no matter how you look at yourself, and no matter how the world may look at you, Jesus looks at you with a love so grand that it's unimaginable to human eyes. He loves you with a love so great that He took the grand step of giving up His life – gladly - so that you may find eternal life with Him. My prayer for you is that you will choose to accept this love, and the invitation to eternal life that comes with it. I can assure you that, with this acceptance of His great love for you, and with a commitment to seek Him first in all that you do, life will take on a joy that you may once have only dreamed of. May God bless you and keep you all!

Acknowledgement

    I have long loved to write, and my husband has long encouraged me to write a book. Because I didn't want to write just any book, I committed to the Lord years ago that I wouldn't write any book unless it was at His direction. Finally, in the early morning hours of March 23, 2011, the Lord prompted me to write a book on prayer. When I woke that morning and started to write, the Lord gave me the entire outline for this book. I wrote no more than 2 hours a day, six days a week for the next 7 weeks, and never came near the computer without first praying that every word I typed would be His and His alone. I did my best to listen to what and when He told me to write, but that is all that I can take credit for in this book. My prayer is that however this book blesses you, that you may see God's Mighty hand in this work, and that all of the credit and the glory would go to God and God alone.

Contents

1. The Power of Prayer 1
2. Your Authority on Earth 9
3. The Power of the Blood 29
4. Hearing His Voice 35
5. Praying in the Will of God 51
6. Breaking Down Roadblocks 85
7. Protection with Prayer 123
8. Praying with others 133
9. Praying for Others 139
10. Verses to Pray With 147

Introduction

In this day and age when it seems as though danger is lurking around every corner, many of us offer up prayers to God for protection, guidance, or deliverance from all of the trouble that life brings us on a daily basis.

Wouldn't it be nice to know whether or not God actually hears your prayers, and that He cares enough to answer? What a relief it would be to know that you really are safe in His arms - that He really does "have your back." So how can you be sure of this?

Do you pray to God? If you pray, do you get answers? Or do you feel as if you are sharing your requests - your *heart* - with a God who may or may not hear you, who may or may not even be there?

How do you know if your prayers will get answered? Are you confident that what you are asking for is His will? Or are you simply offering up your heart, hoping that this Great Big God will have mercy on you?

These are some of the questions that plagued me - and my relationship with God - for many, many years. As I have asked the Lord for wisdom in these areas, He has shared with me some powerful insights into His Word and His will. It is now my privilege to share these insights with you. My hope and my prayer is that it will give you better insight into how prayer works, into who God really is, and into how very much He loves you.

A note to Non-believers: Christians have done a jolly good job of dragging the reputation of Jesus and the Almighty Father God through the mud with a great many acts of hypocrisy, selfishness, hate, anger, violence, and pride. I myself am grateful for the fact that the Lord has allowed me to *write* these words - a gift that comes with the blessing of being able to *erase* and *re-record* - unlike real life or the spoken word, in which I'm sure you'd be able to see the many mistakes I make at the cost of Christ. Christians are called to behave like Christ, but we often screw it up by the way of pride, pain, or simply misunderstanding the Word of God. My prayer for you is that this book will give you insight into the true character of Jesus Christ. He is indeed perfect and full of love for you, and for all of us. Read it with an open heart. You might find something you like in here. ☺

1. The Power of Prayer

Read the following story and ponder in your mind the magnitude of the message:

The next day, as they (Jesus and His disciples) *were leaving Bethany, Jesus was hungry. Seeing in the distance a fig tree in leaf, he went to find out if it had any fruit. When he reached it, he found nothing but leaves, because it was not the season for figs. Then he said to the tree "May no one ever eat fruit from you again." And his disciples heard him say it.* (Mark 11:12-14)

From there, Jesus and His disciples went to Jerusalem, where Jesus rebuked the moneychangers and others whom where selling and buying in the temple courts. We pick up again, the next day, when Jesus and the twelve were heading on to another mission.

In the morning, as they went along, they saw the fig tree (that Jesus had cursed) *withered from the roots. Peter remembered and said to Jesus, "Rabbi, look! The fig tree you cursed has withered!"*

<u>"Have faith in God."</u> Jesus answered. <u>"I tell you the truth, if anyone says to this mountain, 'Go, throw yourself into the sea,' and does not doubt in his heart but believes that what he says will happen, he will have whatever he says.</u> **<u>Therefore I tell you, whatever you ask for in prayer, believe that you have received it, and it will be yours.</u>"** (Mark 11:20-24)

The words that Jesus spoke in the eleventh chapter of Mark are pretty powerful words. Did He really mean that we can have whatever we say? As a person who has always felt called to pray, I used to wonder exactly what, if any, impact prayer really has. I mean, *really -* could simple words, spoken in private or with others, really make a difference?

Did God really even hear my prayers, and if so, would He answer them? My view of God and prayer used to be similar to my view of winning at the slots (for the record, I'm not an advocate of gambling), or of approaching a parent with a request for a new bike or other toy. I knew I had a shot, but how big of a shot was anybody's guess. Would the hearer of my request (mom, dad, the slot machine) have mercy on me, or would I be denied, *again*? Did my requests really even matter, or was God just too busy with bigger fish, like earthquakes, wars and famines?

In August of 2007, I started on a journey to really know this God, whom I had dedicated my life to 12 years earlier, at the age of 28. I wanted to know who He *really* was. There were so many mixed messages out there. Some said God was *this*, and some said He was *that*, but who was right? Was He the "good" God that some said He was? Or was he the "bad" God that others said He was?

I knew that He was in charge, but how could I truly serve Him if I didn't truly know Him? I longed for a closer relationship with God, but I knew in my heart that I couldn't have that closer relationship if I didn't know *His heart*. So I started on a journey to find out just who God was. Through the mentorship of my dear friend Jessie, and through countless hours of reading the Word, I not only found a better understanding of who this God is, but I learned, too, the powerful role prayer plays in the world.

What is Prayer?

Prayer, we know, is our form of communication with God. It's how our spirit speaks to Him and how He speaks to us. Prayer, however, can be so much more than this! This intimate, one-on-one communication with God that we have available to us, when used regularly and done so with a true heart to know Him better, has power beyond words. So what exactly is the power available to us from prayer - what good does it do? Prayer is mentioned in the Bible dozens of times, most often in the New Testament.

The power of prayer and the theme of God's many calls on His people to pray may surprise you.

Prayer has the power to:

-Have God's promise that He is near us: *What other nation [people] is so great as to have their gods near them the way the Lord our God is near us whenever we pray to Him?* (Deuteronomy 4:7)

-Heal entire nations: *If my people, who are called by My Name, will humble themselves and pray and seek my face and turn from their wicked ways, then will I hear from heaven and will forgive their sin and will heal their land.* (2 Chronicles 7:14)

-Grant us mercy: *(My servant Job will pray for you, and I will accept his prayer and not deal with you according to your folly.* (Job 42:8b)

-Keep us from the temptation of sin: <u>*Watch and pray so that you will not fall into temptation. The spirit is willing, but the flesh is weak.*</u> (Mark 14:38)

-The Bible warns that we sin if we don't pray: *As for me, far be it from me that I should sin against the Lord by failing to pray for you.* (1 Samuel 12:23)

-1 Thessalonians 5:17 admonishes us to pray continually.

1. The Power of Prayer

-And the book of James tells us: *"Is any one of you in trouble? He should pray. Is anyone happy? Let him sing songs of praise. Is any one of your sick? He should call the elders of the church to pray over him and anoint him with oil in the name of the Lord. And the prayer offered up in faith will make the sick person well; the Lord will raise him up.* (James 5:13-15).

The verses above are only a fraction of the verses the Word shares with us about prayer. Prayer, it's quite clear, is a powerful weapon for those who know how to use it correctly. It's the most intimate way we have to communicate with the Lord - our own private line to speak with our Father! The 4 gospels speak often of Jesus' many, many hours spent alone, praying to His Father (Luke 5:16, for instance, says that Jesus often withdrew to lonely places to pray). It was the cornerstone of His relationship with God, and it is meant to be the cornerstone of our relationship with God as well. Jesus should be our example when choosing when, where, how, and how much to pray. If the Body of Christ can learn and understand the Word's instructions on successful prayer, we can indeed learn to conquer our adversary, the devil, who *"prowls around like a roaring lion, seeking whom he may devour."* (1 Peter 5:8).

Whatever You Believe

If the above mentioned verses about the fig tree in the book of Mark are true, then prayers do indeed make a difference, and they are certainly powerful. Why is it, then, that we are seeing so very little of our prayers come to pass in the world today?

In order to answer this question, we must first settle the matter of the truth, or non-truth, of God's Word. If you count yourself a Christian, you must decide whether the Bible is the true, spoken Word of God, or whether it is just a guide, put together by well-meaning followers of the Lord. There really is no in-between. If absolute truth exists in the Word of God, then it must exist in the *entire* Word of God, for if you believe one part of the Word is true, and not another, and I believe different verses are true, then there is no absolute truth at all, do you see?

I personally think it's safe to say that the God who created the entire universe and everything in it has the power and capability to assure that His Written Word - *His Guide* - created for all men to show them the path to peace and life, that this God has the power and the capability to assure that His Word remains unaltered. I also believe that there are Bible translators in the history of the world that had hearts committed to hearing the Lord and translating the original versions of the Bible the way God told them to. In fact, the Word itself testifies to this:

All Scripture is given by inspiration of God, and is profitable for doctrine, for reproof, for correction, for instruction in righteousness, that the man of God may be complete, thoroughly equipped for every good work. (2 Timothy 3:16-17)

That being said, we are seeing these days many other "new" versions of the Bible coming out, and let me tell you, they are altering the Word of God in such a way that the authors should be very concerned of the words in the book of Revelation that promises plagues and eternal damnation to anyone who adds to or takes away from the Word of God. God would not have put this warning in the Bible unless He knew that in these end days the Enemy would use people to alter the blessed Word of God.

In my opinion, the King James Version or the New King James Version (KJV OR NKJV) are the most accurate versions of the Bible. I also on occasion use the NIV or the Amplified Bible, often for clarity in verse descriptions. You will find many explanations on the Internet about why one is more accurate than the other, but in my research, I've chosen to stick with the King James Version and the New King James Version. I also prefer older versions, when they can be found, as they tend to stick more to the original texts.

If your spirit is one with Christ, if you are spending sincere time every day with Him in prayer, and if you know the Bible and know it well, you will know full well when reading one of the more "modern" versions of the Bible whether you are reading the truth or not. If you read a verse that is vague, that doesn't sound right, or doesn't make sense, check an older version, and check through your subject guide or concordance for other places in the Word that discuss this same topic. A true verse or concept will be true throughout the Word, not just in one verse. New Christians, or Christians unversed in the Word, get grandma's old King James Version or New King James Version, or consult with an elder, pastor, or other Christian who knows and teaches the truth and has wisdom. These tips will guide you as well into knowing and understanding the Bible. In my humble opinion, however, it's best to stick with the KJV or NKJV.

In order for our prayers to have the most success, they must fall in line with the Word of God, and we can't properly pray in line with the Word if we don't *know* the Word. We'll talk more about this in later chapters, but know that it is one of the main keys to successful prayer.

Prayer is, in my opinion, one of the most underestimated facets of the Christian life. If more people knew and understood what prayer was, and knew of the power behind it, God would get to spend a whole lot more time listening to and answering the prayers of His people. Imagine the change in our world that would follow! Come along with us as we explore the Word and its truths about prayer. Let's see how far your new prayer life will take you.

2. Your Authority on Earth

If you want to have prayers that get results, then you must first understand how prayer works. We talked in the previous chapter about the power of prayer, and about what the Word of God says are some of the things that can be accomplished through prayer. We saw that, just from the example of the fig tree alone, prayer can indeed change things.

So, why is it that some prayers are answered - big and small - and some are not? What is the difference between the pray-ers who see the answers to their prayers, and those who don't?

In order to answer these questions, we must first discern what the Word says about who exactly we are, who exactly Jesus is, and who exactly God is.

Who is God?

In order to have a powerful prayer life, we need to have a clear understanding of Who it is that we are praying to. Just as you cannot have the same true knowledge and intimacy with a stranger as you do with your spouse, you cannot have the fullest relationship with God if you don't have a clear understanding of who He is.

Let's look at the examples of the verses below to give us an idea of who the Bible says God is:

-God is the creator of the heavens and the earth (Genesis 1:1).
-There is no one like God (Exodus 8:10).
-God is jealous for our love (Exodus 20:5).
-God is compassionate, gracious, slow to anger, abounding in love and faithfulness, maintaining His love to thousands, forgiving of wickedness, rebellion and sin (Exodus 34:6-7).
-God is holy; perfect (Leviticus 19:2).
-God is truth (Numbers 23:19).
-God is merciful (Deuteronomy 4:31).
-God is living (Deuteronomy 5:26).
-God keeps His promises (Deuteronomy 7:12).
-God disciplines us out of love (Hebrews 12:6).
-God is greater, bigger than all of us (1 John 4:4).
-God is love (1 John 4:16).

2. Your Authority on Earth

-God is light (1 John 1:5).
-God cannot be tempted by evil (James 1:13).
-God is a consuming fire (Hebrews 12:29).
-God is just (fair) (Hebrews 6:10).
-God created everything for good (1 Timothy 4:4).
-God loves us (Revelation 1:5)!

In a nutshell, God is the Father of all creation - a perfect Father! He loves us more than we could ever comprehend, and since there is no evil in Him, He is able to love and discipline us properly, in a way that will allow us to grow and become more holy, as He calls us to do (Leviticus 11:44). Just as the goal of a parent is to discipline their children in a way that will teach them to learn to obey and follow the correct path, God's goal is to teach us to walk in His way, thereby keeping us from the path of Satan, the Destroyer. (Psalm 17:4)

No one, especially God, wants to see his or her children destroyed or harmed in any way because that child made a wrong choice. Rather, we would have them learn their lessons from small mistakes, and from those, gain the wisdom that allows them to make right choices. That wisdom, however, can only come from *listening* to the instructions of their parents, most of whom have *been there, done that,* and don't want their children to suffer the same ill effects that they themselves suffered for making wrong choices. Although God has never sinned, He is Wisdom, and therefore knows all things, and knows which paths are bad and which are good. This is why an intimate knowledge of God and of His Word is so very, very important to a successful prayer life, and a successful life in general. The Bible contains the answer to every single question we have about how to navigate through life, and how to stay on God's path and off of the path of the Enemy.

The Devil - whether or not we choose to believe in him - is real. God's Word is very clear about that, and it says that Satan comes for one reason: to steal, kill and destroy. Jesus came, however, that we may have life, and life abundantly (John 10:10)! We cannot live in God's promise of an abundant life, however, if we are walking on the Devil's path instead of God's path. That's like following a map to New York, and being angry when you end up there instead of in Florida, where you really wanted to go. If you want to go to Florida, you must follow the path to Florida. The map to New York will never get you there no matter how hard you try.

So many people, even those who are fiercely dedicated to the Lord, suffer needlessly at the hands of the Enemy because they don't recognize his deception, or because they are following the wrong map, or not reading the map at all! Hosea Chapter 4, verse six says *"My people are destroyed from lack of knowledge. Because you reject knowledge, I also reject you as my priests."*

People were given, in God's goodness, a *choice* to learn, embrace and obey God's instructions in His Word, or to reject His knowledge and suffer the consequences. By default, if we don't choose God's way, we fall into the Enemy's path, like it or not. God, though, who outlines thoroughly in Deuteronomy Chapters 28-30 the blessings of following His path and the curses of following the Devil's path, pleads with us to choose *His* path, to *"choose life, that you and your children may live and that you may love the Lord your God, listen to His voice, and hold fast to Him. For the Lord is your life, and he will give you* **many years** *in the land…* (Deuteronomy 30:19-20).

God is love, and He loves us, completely and fully, but true love requires the commitment, the selflessness and the strength to discipline in order to show your children the right path. Choose today to obey your Father in heaven. Embrace His instructions to avoid the Enemy, to heed His discipline and His correction, for it will bring you blessings that you've never even dreamed of!

Who is Jesus?

In the sixth month, God sent the angel Gabriel to Nazareth, a town in Galilee, to a virgin pledged to be married to a man named Joseph, a descendant of David. The virgin's name was Mary. The angel went to her and said "Greetings, you who are highly favored! The Lord is with you." Mary was greatly troubled at his words and wondered what kind of greeting this might be. But the angel said to her, "Do not be afraid, Mary, you have found favor with God. You will be with child and give birth to a son, and you are to give him the name Jesus. **He will be great and will be called the Son of the Most High. The Lord God will give him the throne of his father David, and he will reign over the house of Jacob forever, his kingdom will never end.***"* (Luke 1:26-33)

Jesus, it's clear from many passages in the Bible, was indeed the Son of God. But let's look at some other passages that talk about who God made Jesus to be:

-He is loved by God and pleasing in God's sight (Matthew 3:17, Mark 1:11).
-He is known truly only by God (Matthew 11:27).
-He is THE Christ-the Son of the Living God (Matthew 16:16).
-He is our defender - our mediator, going to the Father on our behalf (1 John 2:1).
-He is The One who will come back for us at the end of days (Matthew 24:30).
-He will come at an hour we don't expect (Matthew 24:44).
-He sits at the right hand of God, his Father (Mark 14:62).
-He came to find, and save, those who are lost (Luke 19:10).
-He is God's one and only true Son (John 3:16).
-He has been sent not to condemn the world, but to save the world (John 3:17)
-He has been granted authority over all people in order to give them eternal life (John 17:2).
-He was raised from the dead (1 Corinthians 15:20).
-He is one with the Father (John 10:30)
-He is our rescuer (1 Thessalonians 1:10).
-He is the only way to God (John 14:6).
-He loves us (John 15:12)!

Jesus, it's clear, is the true Son of God Almighty, our Father in heaven. Our Father in heaven sent Jesus to restore the authority on earth that we lost when the Devil convinced Adam and Eve to disobey God's rules and commit the first sin here on earth. We'll talk more about why

2. Your Authority on Earth

Jesus had to come later on in the chapter. Let's first talk, however, about who we are as adopted sons and daughters of the Most High God.

Who we are in Christ

Now that we have a better understanding of who God is, and of who Jesus is, it's time to find out just who *we* are as a part of the body of Christ.

If you read the Word, it's very evident that Jesus ranks pretty high up there in the realm of authority. The book of Psalms gives us clear evidence on the coming reign of Jesus in the second chapter:

<u>I have installed my King on Zion, my holy hill</u>. I will proclaim the decree of the Lord: He said to me "<u>You are my Son, today I have become your Father. Ask of me, and I will make the nations your inheritance, the ends of the earth your possession. You will rule them with an iron scepter; you will dash them to pieces like pottery</u>." Therefore, you kings, be wise; be warned, you rulers of the earth. Serve the Lord with fear and rejoice with trembling. Kiss the Son, lest he be angry and you be destroyed in your way, for His wrath can flare up in a moment. Blessed are all who put their trust in Him. (Psalm 2:6-12)

Now, I'm not sure about you, but this does not sound like a king that I want to mess with. It's evident that He indeed does have the authority to do whatever it is He decides to do. I think I'll be the one "who puts their trust in Him" as opposed to the one who will be "destroyed in my way".

I'm not sharing this particular passage with you to scare you - in fact you have nothing to fear if you've made Jesus the Lord of your life. In order to understand *your* authority here on earth, however, you must first understand *His* authority here on earth. The book of Psalms says about Jesus that God *"crowned Him with glory and honor, made Him ruler over the works of His* (God's) *hands, and put everything under his feet."* (Psalms 8:5-6)

Those verses help to make clear Jesus' authority here on earth. So, how do we fit in? Let's look at Genesis 1: 26-28:

Then God said "Let us (Father, Son, Holy Spirit) *make man in our image, in our likeness, and let them rule over the fish of the sea and the birds of the air, over the livestock, over all the earth, and over all the creatures that move along the ground."*

This clarifies where we as humans are in the lineup of all the creatures on earth. We are first after The Father, Son, and Holy Spirit - no doubt about it. So, where does Jesus fit in?

Paul says in First Corinthians, "Now I want you to realize that the head of *every man* is Christ, and the head of the woman is man, and the head of Christ is God."

Christ is the Son of God, and God, in His sovereignty, gave Christ rule over the world:

All authority in heaven and on earth has been given to me. (Matthew 28:18)

2. Your Authority on Earth

Now, the really good news is that we - you, me, and everyone else who accepts Jesus as their Savior, have been adopted by God as children because of Jesus' sacrifice on the cross! Let's look and see what God's promises are to us as followers of Christ:

-Romans 8:17 says that receivers of salvation are *"heirs of God and co-heirs with Christ…"*

-In Second Corinthians 6:18 God says <u>I shall be a Father to you, and you shall be my sons and daughters.</u>

-First John 3:1 tells us *"Behold, what manner of love the Father has bestowed on us, that we should be called children of God!"*

-And Galatians 4:5-6 gives us an even better description of the authority that comes with being a son or daughter of Jesus Christ:

But when the time had fully come, God sent His Son, born of a woman, born under law, to redeem those under law, that we might **receive the full rights of sons***. Because you are sons, God sent the Spirit of His Son into our hearts, the Spirit who calls out <u>"Abba, Father".</u> So you are no longer a slave* (to the Enemy)*, but a son; and since you are a son, God has made you also an heir.*

Jesus is King of kings, and Lord of Lords. His Father, the Almighty God, with His authority, made Christ the King of Kings. How blessed we are to be welcomed into this Most

Holy family as brothers and sisters in Christ and sons and daughters – heirs - of the Most High God!

Why Jesus?

Now, I want to stop here and talk a bit about sin, and why there's a need for a Savior such as Jesus Christ. This was, for years, confusing to me. If God *really* loved us, why couldn't He just forgive us and get it over with? Why the need for Jesus to die His horrible death on the cross and why do we have to choose to follow Jesus to be forgiven?

An explanation that you may best understand is one that many of you have encountered, either first hand or second hand, lots of times:

In your home, you have rules, correct? Things like *pick up after yourselves, treat people with respect, take out the garbage*, or whatever it is that your family rules are. If the people in your household were allowed to ignore these rules, say a simple "I'm sorry." (heartfelt or not) and go on ignoring these rules, your house would be in utter chaos. The people living in it would soon become selfish and self-serving and void of any empathy or understanding of how their actions affected others. It's obvious that this type of a living situation would create a terrible outcome, as the members of the family would then go and spread their self-serving acts and hard-heartedness throughout their community and world.

We've all seen or met children, or adults, who have never had consequences for their actions. They are extremely difficult to be around, and many times cause lots of pain, as their concern is only for themselves.

Now, God is the Most Wonderful, Most Merciful, Most Loving being in the Universe. He is Creator of All Things. He is also perfect. With that perfect spirit, there must be justice and judgment. Without it, He would not be perfect. A perfect God does not let crimes against Himself and His people go unpunished. How sad is it when a child hits or otherwise hurts a sibling and his or her parents ignore the act? What message does that send to the injured child? It tells them that they are not important, and that their feelings and well-being do not matter.

You see, if God were to ignore our wrongs, without providing some type of correction, some type of justification for the wronged party, He wouldn't be a perfect God at all. When discipline is administered correctly, however, it teaches us empathy, compassion, and it teaches how we need to behave in order to live a more peaceful life.

When Adam and Eve first came upon the earth by God's hand, they were perfect - without sin. When, however, Eve was deceived by the serpent and chose to listen to his lies, and Adam chose to follow her prompting to go along with her in this sin, they separated themselves from God. They chose disunity with God and unity with another god - a false god - thereby giving him (the Devil) the authority over the earth that had been given them by God (Genesis 1:26). After they realized what they had done, of course, they were devastated, but it was too late - the damage had been done.

As God loved Adam and Eve with all of His heart, He too wanted to have that unity with man back again. But the only consequence worthy of such a sin would be the sacrifice of a perfect being - someone who, like God, was perfect, to make atonement (payment for the debt of sin) for what Adam, and all of mankind after him, had done as sinners.

Since the payment had to be made to God - he was the debtor - He needed a perfect being other than Himself to be that atonement, or payment. So He sent His beloved Son, Jesus, down to earth as a man. Because man has been given authority over the earth, and sin came through man, sin also had to be atoned for through man:

For since by man came death (through sin), *by Man also came the resurrection of the dead. For as in Adam all die, even so in Christ all shall be made alive.* (1 Corinthians 15:21-22)

Jesus' main purpose on earth was to be convicted and killed on the cross for debts that were not His in order to gain back the unity with God that you and I lost when Adam and Eve gave our authority to Satan. So, He walked His 33 years here, all without sin, and in God's timing, the powers that be on this earth sentenced Him to die on the cross.

This perfect sacrifice wiped sin out for all time. It washed sin away, like a flooding river washes away everything in its path. Jesus' sacrifice washed away every sin that ever was, and every sin that ever would be. It forgave us for all of our sins, allowing for God to see us through the perfect lens of the Perfect Jesus.

Likewise, the people who choose to accept Jesus' gift, have Jesus as their Savior and choose to turn away from their own path have their sins washed away too, forever! Isn't that wonderful news?

The Honors and Benefits of Following Jesus

There's more good news, however! Once you choose to accept Jesus as the leader of your life, you inherit the honors and benefits of being the son of the King! Look around at all of the media buzz about Prince William and his upcoming nuptials, which are about a month away at this writing. This wouldn't be nearly as exciting if Prince William lived in abject poverty, but as heir of the throne of England, he doesn't have to. He is entitled to the honors and riches of the family of the Queen.

Those who have decided to follow Jesus Christ have inherited many more honors and benefits - benefits that come with being a child of the Most High God.

What are some of those benefits? First and foremost, we have eternal life as opposed to eternal damnation - the consequence for those who have decided to turn away from God and live in the Enemy's world:

For God so loved the world that He gave His one and only Son, that whosoever believes in Him shall not perish but have everlasting life. For God did not send His Son into the world to condemn the world, but to save the world through Him. (John 3:16-17)

Secondly, the shedding of Jesus' blood for our sins made us righteous in God's sight. The definition of the word "righteous" in Webster's Dictionary is *upright*, as in perfect, or, walking perfectly. Now, you and I both know that there is not one person on this earth that is truly righteous, or without sin, and the Bible confirms it:

> *As it is written: "There is no one righteous, no even one."* (Romans 3:10)
> *for all have sinned and fall short of the glory of God* (Romans 2:23)

Yet, praise the Lord, Christ purchased righteousness for us!

> *We implore you on Christ's behalf: Be reconciled to God. God made Him who had no sin to be sin for us, so that in Him we might become the righteousness of God.* (2 Corinthians 5:20-21)

It is fact that when we choose to have Jesus Christ as the leader of our lives, that through Jesus Christ, we are made righteous, in spite of our sins, and that righteousness is what allows us to go "boldly before the throne of God to obtain help and grace" in our time of need (Hebrews 4:16). It is that righteousness that gives us the authority and the right to go to God in prayer and be welcomed into His sight.

Another benefit we received for being sons and daughters of God is the power and authority that Jesus had here on earth. Jesus proved His authority and His power here on earth time and time again through the many miracles He performed here. Let's take a look at some of those showings of His authority:

When Jesus came down from the mountainside, large crowds followed Him. A man with leprosy came to Jesus and knelt before Him and said "Lord, if you are willing, you can make me clean." Jesus reached out His hand and touched the man. <u>"I am willing,"</u> he said. <u>"Be clean!"</u> Immediately the man was cured of his leprosy. (Matthew 8:1-3)

When Jesus came into Peter's house, he saw Peter's mother-in-law lying in bed with a fever. He touched her hand and the fever left her, and she got up and began to wait on Him. When evening came, many who were demon-possessed were brought to Him and He drove out the spirits with a word and healed all the sick. (Matthew 8:14-16)

When Jesus landed on the other side and saw a large crowd, he had compassion on them, because they were like sheep without a shepherd. So he began teaching them many things. By this time it was late in the day, so His disciples came to Him. "This is a remote place," they said, "and it's already very late. Send the people away so they can go to the surrounding countryside and villages and buy themselves something to eat." But Jesus answered, <u>"You give them something to eat."</u> They said to Him, "That would take eight months of a man's wages! Are we to go and spend that much on bread and give it to them to eat?" <u>"How many loaves do you have?"</u> Jesus asked. "Five - and two fish." They answered. Then Jesus directed them to have all the people sit down in groups on the grass. So they sat down in groups of hundreds and fifties.

Taking the five loaves and the two fish and looking up to heaven, He gave thanks and broke the loaves. Then he gave them to his disciples to set before the people. He also divided the two fish among them all. They all ate and were satisfied, and the disciples picked up twelve basketfuls of broken pieces of bread and fish. The number of men who had eaten was **five thousand**. (Mark 6:34-44)

Now when Jesus returned, a crowd welcomed Him, for they were all expecting Him. Then a man named Jairus, a ruler of the synagogue, came and fell at Jesus' feet, pleading with Him to come to his house, because his only daughter, a girl of about twelve, was dying. As Jesus was on His way, the crowds almost crushed Him. And a woman was there who had been subject to bleeding for twelve years, but no one could heal her. She came up behind Him and touched the edge of His cloak, and immediately her bleeding stopped. <u>"Who touched me?"</u> Jesus asked. When they all denied it, Peter said "Master, the people are all crowding against you." But Jesus <u>said "Someone touched me; I know that power has gone out from me."</u> Then the woman, seeing that she could not go unnoticed, came trembling and fell at His feet. In the presence of all the people, she told why she had touched Him and how she had been instantly healed. Then He said to her <u>"Daughter, your faith has healed you. Go in peace."</u> While Jesus was still speaking, someone came from the house of Jairus and said, "Your daughter is dead. Don't bother the teacher anymore." Hearing this, Jesus said to Jairus <u>"Don't be afraid; just believe, and she will be healed."</u> When Jesus arrived at the house of Jairus, He did not let anyone go in with Him except Peter, John, James, and the child's father and mother. Meanwhile all of *the people were wailing and mourning for her. <u>"Stop wailing,"</u> Jesus said. <u>"She is not dead, but asleep."</u> They laughed at Him, knowing she was dead. But Jesus took her by the hand and said, <u>"My child, get up!"</u> Her spirit returned and at once she stood up. Then Jesus told her parents to give her something to eat.* (Luke 8:40-55)

Jesus proved His authority while He was on earth by doing many, many miracles - from a simple turning of water into wine (John 2:1-11) to raising people like Jairus' daughter and Lazarus from the dead.

So, how does Jesus' authority affect us? Let's start with a look at the gospel of John. In the 14th chapter, Jesus shares the greatness of His authority with the disciples. Let's read what He has to say, starting in verse 11:

<u>*Believe me when I say that I am in the Father and the Father is in me; or at least believe on the evidence of the miracles themselves. I tell you the truth, anyone who has faith in me will do what I have been doing. He will do even* **greater** *things than these, because I am going to the Father. And I will do whatever you ask in my name, so that the Son may bring glory to the Father. You may ask me for anything in my name, and I will do it.*</u> (John 14:11-14)

That sounds like a pretty good deal, doesn't it? So, why would God want to give us a deal like that? There are two main reasons that I have found in the Word for this great "deal". The first example is found in the seventh chapter of Matthew:

Which of you, if his son asks for bread, will give him a stone? Or if he asks for a fish, will give him a snake? If you, then, though you are evil (sinners)*, know how to give good gifts to your children, how much more will your Father in heaven give good gifts to those who ask Him!* (Matthew 7:9-11)

The first reason for God's pouring of blessings out on us is that He *loves* us, and with a love so great that it is incomprehensible to human hearts! The second reason, of course, is The Great Commission.

Therefore go and make disciples of all nations, baptizing them in the name of the Father and of the Son and of the Holy Spirit, and teaching them to obey everything I have commanded you. (Matthew 28:19-20)

The Bible is clear that it is God's will for "*all men to be saved and to come to a knowledge of the Truth.*" (1 Timothy 2:3-4)

We know from the Word that Jesus' first reason for coming to earth was to save the people. We also know that He came to glorify God.

What better glorifies God than the world seeing how wonderful He is, and what better way for unbelievers to be drawn to Christ than by seeing evidence of the overwhelming goodness of God?

In Jeremiah 29:11, the Lord says, *"For I know the plans I have for you-plans to prosper and not harm you, plans to give you a future and a hope."*

2. Your Authority on Earth

You see, by giving you and I the authority through Christ Jesus to accomplish miracles and to get our prayers answered, Jesus helps to get His will accomplished: saving His people from the hands of the Enemy, and bringing His Father glory. Hallelujah, let it be so!

God has ordained us all to be a part of the Body of Christ. We all, with the authority given us by God, have our appointed jobs to do in bringing the love of Christ to the unsaved, so that every single person on earth will hear about Jesus, and, hopefully, accept Jesus into their hearts as their Lord and Savior, thereby taking their places at the feast with Abraham, Isaac and Jacob in the kingdom of Heaven. (Matthew 8:11). So let's get to work!

3.
The Power of the Blood

One of the key factors to truly understanding Jesus, His authority, and our unlimited use of that authority through Him, is for us to understand what power lies in the shedding of His blood for us.

What does the Bible say about Jesus' blood, and blood in general? God first talks to us about blood when He speaks to Noah after the flood in Genesis chapter 9, verse 6:

"Whoever sheds the blood of man, by man shall his blood be shed; for in the image of God has God made man."

This is a pretty strong warning, not just about our blood, but about our value in God's eyes as men and women made in His image. Again, we see authority here - the high value God has given us as His people.

We see a second example of the power of blood in Exodus, when God was preparing His people to be taken from under Pharoah's control, and the plague of death was coming upon the Egyptians because of Pharoah's unwillingness to release the Israelites:

"<u>Take some of the blood (from a sacrificial lamb) and put it on the sides and tops of the doorframes of the houses where they eat the lambs…… On that same night, I will pass through Egypt and strike down every firstborn - both men and animals - and I will bring judgment on all the gods of Egypt, for I am the Lord. The blood will be a sign for you on the houses where you are; and when I see the blood, I will pass over you. No destructive plague will touch you when I strike Egypt.</u>" (Exodus 12:7, 12, 13)

The application of the blood here literally saved the lives of thousands of people and animals. It was a symbol for the people - God's promise to them of protection and redemption.

God also used blood to make His covenants with the people of Israel when He first shared His laws with them after He delivered them from slavery, and He used blood through circumcision when He confirmed His covenant with Abraham.

Psalm 72:14 says *"He will rescue them (His people) from oppression and violence, for precious is their blood in His sight."*

Leviticus 17:11 says *"The life of a creature is in its blood"*

God says in Proverbs 6:17 that hands that shed innocent blood are detestable to Him.

It's clear from the Word that the Lord, from the beginning, placed quite a high value on blood. He used blood to establish His covenants in the Old Testament, and He used the blood of His Son Jesus to establish His eternal covenant with the people on earth who choose to enter into that covenant with Him. Now let's take a further look at how the value of the blood of His son was so important in establishing an eternal covenant to save people from an eternity in Hell.

When Jesus took the first communion with His disciples, He made His purpose on earth clear as He explained the symbolism of the act of communion as a remembrance of His shed blood for our sins:

<u>*"Drink from it, all of you. This is my blood of the covenant, which is poured out for many for the forgiveness of sins."*</u> (Matthew 26:27b-28)

Ephesians 1:7 says, *"In Him, we have redemption through His blood, the forgiveness of sins, in accordance with the riches of God's grace...."*

Ephesians 2:13 says that: *But now in Christ Jesus you who once were far away have been brought near through the blood of Christ.*

Colossians 1:20 says that we are reconciled to God by the making of peace through Christ's blood, shed on the cross.

Hebrews 9:22 says that without the shedding of blood there can be no forgiveness of sins.

And 1 Peter 1:18-21 says *"for you know that it was not with perishable things such as silver or gold that you were redeemed from the empty way of life handed down to you from your forefathers, but with the precious blood of Christ, a lamb without blemish or defect. He was chosen before the creation of the world but was revealed in these last times for your sake. Through Him you believe in God, who raised Him from the dead and glorified Him, and so your faith and hope are in God."*

1 John 1:7 says that the blood of Jesus purifies us from all sin.

Revelation 5:9 says that Jesus was slain, and with His blood He purchased for God men from every nation and tribe on earth, and in chapter 12, verse 11, it says that we, the people who've accepted Jesus as our Savior, have *overcome* the Accuser (Satan) by the blood of the Lamb!

Can you see the power and value God puts on blood - especially the Blood of His precious Son?

3. The Power of the Blood

Now let's talk a little bit about the word "covenant." In Noah Webster's 1828 Dictionary, he defines the word covenant as "God's promise to man". When God makes a covenant, you can bet your money that the terms of that covenant will be carried out. In Titus 1:2 it says that God cannot lie.

Every time in the Bible when God made a life changing promise, He uses the word "covenant". A covenant is the granddaddy of all promises - an agreement that is never meant to be broken.

When God sent His Son to shed His own blood for our sins, He was buying back all of the authority that man lost when Adam sided with Satan in the Garden of Eden. All of the promises of the Devil; sickness, sin, and all of the other garbage that the Enemy puts upon us or tries to put upon us was bought back by Jesus' shedding of the Blood on the cross! Revelation 1:18 confirms this when Jesus tells us:

I am the Living One; I was dead, and behold I am alive forever and ever! And I hold the keys of death and Hades.

He shows us in Matthew 16:19 where He allows man, through His victory, to share in this authority as well!

"I will give you the keys of the kingdom of heaven; whatever you bind on earth will be bound in heaven, and whatever you loose on earth will be loosed in heaven."

The Blood of Jesus is not only our ticket out of hell, but the restoration of the high place man was meant to have from the beginning - a place of authority as a son of God in the Body of Christ! The shedding of Jesus' blood is what allows us to "*come boldly before the throne of grace, that we may receive mercy and find grace to help us in our time of need.*" (Hebrews 4:16)!

Therefore, let us always remember the great power and authority we have been given through the shedding of Jesus' blood. It will allow us to go to God *confidently* in prayer, knowing that, by the Blood, we are His chosen sons and daughters!

4. Hearing His Voice

Hearing God's voice is another crucial element to answered prayer, and God's protection in general. So why is it that some people seem to hear God's voice so clearly, and others don't seem to hear it at all? Is hearing God's voice a privilege only granted to some?

Jesus says in the book of John that believers will indeed know His voice. Read here as He talks about His role as the Good Shepherd of His people:

<u>I tell you the truth, the man who does not enter the sheep pen by the gate, but climbs in by some other way, is a thief and a robber. The man who enters by the gate is the shepherd</u>

> *of his sheep. The watchman opens the gate for him, and the sheep listen to his voice. He calls his own sheep by name and leads them out. When he has brought out all his own, he goes on ahead of them, and his sheep follow him because they **know his voice**.* (John 10:1-4)

> *I am the good shepherd. I know my sheep and my sheep know me - just as the Father knows me and I know the Father - and I lay down my life for the sheep. I have other sheep too that are not of this sheep pen. I must bring them also. **They too will listen to my voice**, and there will be one flock and one shepherd.* (John 10:14-16)

Jesus has made it clear that His people know His voice. Why is it, then, that some of us have such a hard time hearing? If we cannot hear His voice, are we not *true* believers? Have we "missed the boat" so to speak?

You can be comforted to know that hearing God is a gift that is available to all who have truly committed their lives to Christ. It is a gift, however, that often takes time to develop. Just as it takes time after you marry to know the many different facets of your spouse, knowing God and hearing His voice requires that you spend time with Him, and that you work hard at learning to know Him.

A Willingness to Listen

In order to hear the voice of God, you must first *choose to listen*. God is clear in the Bible that this is one of the key elements of our protection and blessing in Him:

4. Hearing His Voice

*This day I call heaven and earth as witnesses against you that I have set before you life and death, blessings and curses. Now **choose life**, so that you and your descendants may live and that you may love the Lord your God, **listen to His voice,** and hold fast to Him.* (Deuteronomy 30:19-20)

He admonishes us again in the book of James about listening:

*My dear brothers, take note of this: Everyone should be **quick to listen**, slow to speak and slow to become angry, for man's anger does not bring about the righteous life that God desires.* (James 1:19-20)

Now listening, believe it or not, is an art. It takes practice, and it takes wisdom. Because we were born with a sin nature, we are so used to focusing on ourselves and getting what *we* want that we naturally do a lot more talking than we do listening. So learning to be a listener requires prayer, patience, and a willingness for people to *"no longer live for themselves but for him who died for them and was raised again."* (2 Corinthians 5:15)

The Bible makes it clear that talking, as opposed to listening, brings great trouble upon the world anyway. Let's look at some of the verses that show us how too much talking and not enough listening can get us into trouble:

He who answers before listening - that is his folly and his shame (Proverbs 18:13).

Better is a poor man whose walk is blameless than a fool whose lips are perverse (Proverbs 19:1).

He who guards his lips guards his life, but he who speaks rashly will come to ruin (Proverbs 13:3).

How many times have you said something before thinking and prayed with all of your heart that you could take it back? It's happened to me more times than I care to remember. Unfortunately, there's no "rewind" in real life. Once those words are out there, the damage has been done, and although an apology might help ease the pain, the memory of those harsh or hurtful words will replay over and over in the recipient's minds. That's one of the many tactics the Enemy uses to keep people hurting and therefore hindering the spreading of the love of God.

Many of you have heard the story of the father who used his fence to teach his child of this truth:

> One day a father took his son out back to the wooden fence in the yard. He handed his son a bucket of nails and a hammer, and said to him "Son, I want you to hammer all of these nails into the fence." The son completed his task, and then went to his father for further instruction. The father said "Son, now I would like you to take all of the nails out of the fence, and put them back in the bucket." The son was confused, and a bit annoyed by these instructions, but finished the job and brought the bucket of nails back to his father. "Now, son," the father said, "I want you to look at all of the holes in this

fence. These holes are a representation of the harsh words we speak and the hurtful things that we can do. When you say and do things that hurt others, you can always, and should always, go back and apologize. But the wound, although improved, will always remain, just as the holes in this fence will always remain. Remember this lesson, and be certain to speak and act kindly to all of those around you."

This story has for many years been a reminder to me to continue to work at disciplining my words and my actions. When we learn to listen *first* and when we're slow to speak, we gain the wisdom to know what words will build up instead of tear down.

Now let's read about some of the verses that show us what blessings listening will bring:

*A wise man will **hear and increase learning,** and a man of understanding will attain wise counsel.* (Proverbs 1:5).

*The way of a fool seems right to him, but a wise man **listens** to advice* (Proverbs 12:15).

In the book of 1 Samuel, when Samuel was about to be anointed as a prophet of the Lord, he got that blessing in large part because he chose to *listen* to God when He spoke to him. When Samuel heard God's voice, he said *"Speak, Lord, I am **listening."*** (1 Samuel 3:10). This showed the Lord that He had Samuel's heart, and that He could trust Samuel to obey His instructions.

Having a willingness to listen, then, is the first key in having the ability to hear God's voice.

Know Him, Know His Voice

Just as mothers know the cry of their child in a crowd, and just as a child knows the call of their mother's (or father's) voice, we must learn to recognize the voice of our Father. A child knows his parent's voice, and a parent knows his child's voice, because they *know* each other. They spend time together - many hours a day, especially when the children are smaller. The same rules apply to hearing God's voice. You cannot recognize the voice of a stranger, and despite the many myths out there, God does not often roll in yelling and thundering and forcing us to hear Him speak.

The prophet Elijah learned this firsthand. King Ahab and his queen, Jezebel, were among the most evil of all of the kings and queens in the Bible. After Elijah had made a great show of the power of the Lord God and a great fool of the queen's false prophets, suffice to say the queen's next mission was to take his life. This put Elijah at the end of his rope, so to speak, so Elijah ran to escape her wrath. He ended up, after many days, in a cave on Mount Sinai. We pick up the story in the Word with a frustrated and very much feeling-defeated Elijah:

And the word of the Lord came to him: <u>*"What are you doing here, Elijah?*</u> *He replied, "I have been very zealous for the Lord God Almighty. The Israelites have rejected your covenant, broken down your altars, and put your prophets to* *death with the sword. I am the only one left, and now they are trying to kill me too!" The Lord said, "<u>Go out and stand on the mountain in the presence of the Lord, for the Lord is about to pass by.</u>" Then a great and powerful wind tore the mountains apart and shattered the rocks before the Lord, but the Lord was not in the wind. After the wind there was an earthquake, but the Lord was not in the earthquake. After the earthquake came a fire, but the Lord was not in the fire. And after the fire,* ***a still, small voice****.* (1 Kings 19:9-12)

Praise God, He delivered Elijah, and eventually gave him an assistant and a successor in the prophet Elisha. But Elijah first had to discern the Lord's voice so he could *hear* the Lord's instructions - His still, small voice.

I've been hearing the Lord's voice for over two decades now, and only twice in all that time has His inaudible voice been "loud". Once was when I was in terrible danger and didn't realize it, and the other time was when I was praying, or should I say *nagging*, to God repeatedly for a blessing for one of my brothers who first needed to be prayed for to receive salvation. Every other time He has spoken to me, it's been in that still, small voice, and in order to hear that still, small voice, you have got to be *listening*! If you're too busy talking, your chatter will drown the voice of the Lord out!

The Lord knows you inside and out. The Word says in Jeremiah 1:5 *"Before I formed you in the womb I knew you."* We need to *ask* the Lord for what we want, simply because God is a gentleman, and He will not force His way into our lives, but He knows what you want and need before you even ask (Matthew 6:8)! We, however, need to choose to get to know Him before we can really *hear* Him. He is a gracious and loving God who wants to bless His children and be there for them. Learn to be quiet in His presence, choose to spend time with him, learn to really know Him, and you will learn to hear His voice. Believe me; He has great and exciting things to share with you!

Knowing His Word

Knowing His Word is another very important part in being able to discern the Lord's voice. The Devil is the Great Deceiver. He knows the Word of God very well, and yes, he does a very good imitation of God's still, small voice. So how can we be sure that we are hearing God instead of the Enemy? It starts with knowing His Word, and the best way to *know* His Word is to spend *time* in His Word.

With all of the things on our "to do" list these days, it's very easy to get caught up into thinking you don't have time to spend in the Word and in prayer. However, just as your car, your health, and your family can't go for long periods without time and care, neither can your spirit. Oh, the Enemy will do a stellar job of convincing you that you're doing fine. That unrest you feel, however, deep down in your spirit - that anxiousness, and that agitation - that comes from a *need*. **It comes from a need to have time alone with your Savior.** Just as you need alone time with your spouse, and alone time with each of your children, you need that same alone time with God. It allows for you to reconnect and close up those gaps of separation that the world and its busyness create.

4. Hearing His Voice

Why is it so important that we spend time alone with God in prayer and in His Word? God says in His Word: *"For my thoughts are not your thoughts, neither are your ways my ways. As the heavens are higher than the earth, so are my ways higher than your ways, and my thoughts than your thoughts."* (Isaiah 55:8-9)

Does this mean that God does not want us to know His thoughts and ways? Absolutely not! Most of us, though, spend so little time truly studying the Word that we don't have a clue about His desires for us and our lives, and we cannot discern His voice if we do not know His Word and know His thoughts and ways.

I am spending more time in the Bible now than I ever have, and I am still continually amazed at what the Lord shows me about who He is. His love for us is so big that I am, after a couple of years now of spending every morning in the Word and many times throughout the day in prayer, only now starting to see the tip of the iceberg in regards to His great love for us.

I would say that by far the best piece of spiritual advice I've ever gotten was the advice to get up early in the morning and spend my first minutes with the Lord. It has changed my life exponentially. I am nicer, happier, mentally more alert and stronger, and I have acquired a level of peace that far surpasses any I've known before. Spending time in the morning with the Lord first - before you do anything else - is kind of like having a good, healthy breakfast. It gives you an extra boost to get you through your day!

I realize that this can seem like an uncomfortable thing to do if you're not used to prayer and time alone with God. If that's the case, start small. Get up before anyone else is up. Grab a cup of coffee, read a few verses from the Word, and say a quick prayer. Start small, and you'll soon notice that your days are going better, and you'll crave your time with God! And no, *ending* your days with God is not the same as *starting* them with God. Yes, it's wonderful to have your time with God right before bed, and you *should* do this, but give Him your first fruits too - your tithe on your day. It's a way of showing Him that He is indeed first in your life, and it will bless you more than you can imagine. Better yet, as your time in the Word and in fellowship with God increases, you'll better be able to discern the Lord's voice, because you know His thoughts and His ways!

Learn to Discern

Another big part of hearing the Lord's voice is recognizing the voice of the Enemy. Remember that Satan was once known as Lucifer, God's highest ranking angel. The Devil knows the Word inside and out, and he also knows how to twist the Word to deceive God's people. The Enemy has such a thorough knowledge of the Word of God that he has even mastered the ability to speak to our spirits in an imitation of the still, small voice that our Lord uses. This is why it's so important that when you hear something, you know without a doubt which camp that word is coming from.

Jesus Himself had to deal with the Enemy's mastery of deception where God's Word is concerned during His walk here on earth as a man. Remember that God cannot be tempted by the Devil. The book of James says:

When tempted, no one should say, "God is tempting me." For God cannot be tempted by evil, nor does He tempt anyone;" (James 1:13)

Since Jesus had to come down to earth as a man, however, in order to be subject to the same temptations that you and I face, He was tempted by the Devil. Let's see how Jesus handled this:

Then Jesus was led by the Spirit into the desert to be tempted by the Devil. After fasting forty days and forty nights, He was hungry. The Tempter came to Him and said, ""f you are the Son of God, tell these stones to become bread." Jesus answered, <u>'It is written: "Man does not live by bread alone, but by every word that comes from the mouth of God."'</u> Then the Devil took Him to the holy city and had Him stand on the highest point of the temple. "If you are the Son of God," he said, "throw yourself down. For it is written:

> *"'He will command His angels concerning you, and they will lift you up in their hands, so that you will not strike your foot against a stone."'*

Jesus answered him <u>"It is also written: 'Do not put the Lord your God to the test.'"</u> Again the Devil took Him to a very high mountain and showed Him all the kingdoms of the world and their splendor. "All this I will give you," he said, "if you will bow down and worship me." Jesus said to him, <u>"Away from me, Satan! For it is written: 'Worship the Lord your God and</u>

serve Him only.'" Then the Devil left Him and angels came and attended Him. (Matthew 4:1-11)

Now, it's important to notice three things about this passage:

1. The Enemy knew the Word, and he knew it well.
2. The Enemy knew how to twist the Word in an attempt to deceive the hearer.
3. Jesus knew the Word better than the Enemy, and therefore was able to trump the Devil's tactics.

The most important way we can discern between the Enemy's voice and God's voice is to have a completely thorough knowledge of the Word of God. Every word in the Bible is there so that God's people have the knowledge they need to overcome the Enemy and have victory in Christ. You can know the love of Jesus, you can pray, you can do good works, more than all the peoples on the face of the earth, but without intimate knowledge of the Word of God, you are wandering aimlessly without a map! You cannot truly know His will unless you know His Word - that's why He gave it to us! The book of Hebrews tells us that:

The Word of God is living and active. Sharper than any two-edged sword, it penetrates even to dividing soul and spirit, joints and marrow; (Hebrews 4:12).

And the book of Ephesians tells us to:

Take the helmet of salvation and the sword of the Spirit, which is the Word of God; praying always with all prayer and supplication in the Spirit, being watchful to this end... (Ephesians 6:17-18).

The Word of God is by far our most powerful weapon against the Enemy, and our most powerful weapon in learning to discern the difference between the voice of God and the voice of the Devil. Notice in the above passage where Jesus is tempted that He knew the Word so well that not only was He able to recognize when the Enemy was twisting God's Word, He was also able to counter the Enemy's tactics by using the Word as a sword to shut the mouth of the Enemy and drive him away.

Knowing the Word well enough to know when the Devil is twisting it to deceive you requires that you spend time in the Word, and regularly. The Bible talks about the Word of God as food for our souls. No one, by choice, goes without food every day unless they are setting a time of fasting, which is temporary. Likewise, we should "feed" our spirits every single day with the Word of God. The Word of God is crucial to:

Defending ourselves from the Enemy (Matthew 4:1-11)
Building our faith (Romans 10:17)
Nourishing our spirits (Deuteronomy 8:3)
Keeping us from sin (Psalm 119:9, 11)
Showing us the way to go (Psalm 119:105)

and to our entire walk in this world. Having had a life without God, and without the Word, I don't know quite how I survived during those times. It was certainly by the grace of God. I continually made bad choices and walked on paths where I shouldn't have been. I was ignorant - a sheep wandering aimlessly without a shepherd, trying to make it on my own. How blessed are those who choose to study the Word of God and have that roadmap to show them the way!

Make time, every day, to spend in the Word. Every good nutritionist will tell you that a good, healthy breakfast is essential to giving your physical body the strength it needs to do all that you ask it to do every day. In the same way, filling your body with the Word in the morning will give you the strength and encouragement and the wisdom you need to navigate through the snares and traps the Devil lays for us on a daily basis. When you commit to this regular routine of feeding your spirit with the Word, hearing His voice, and discerning it from the voice of the Enemy, hearing God will become so routine and automatic that it will be the same as talking to your spouse, your kids or anyone else. You will learn that you can hear quickly and obey immediately and automatically.

Our family got to experience the benefits of this regular feeding on the Word not too long ago on a car drive with my kids. We were approaching a 4-way stop in which both roads had speed limits of 55 miles per hour. I stopped, and with no one waiting at the signs going the other way, would have normally proceeded through the sign, but the Lord immediately spoke to me. *Wait.* Having gotten better at hearing His voice through the reading of the Word, I immediately obeyed. I looked, and saw approaching on my left a distracted driver that obviously didn't see the sign and had no intention of slowing down. At 55 miles per hour, he came to and passed through the intersection quite fast, and didn't slow down or realize what he had done until about 100 feet after he'd blown through that stop sign. I know that in the "olden days" before the Word of God had been planted in my heart, I would have looked no further than the intersection, proceeded through that sign, as was my right, and been t-boned at 55 mph with my kids in the car. The results for all involved would've been disastrous. Thanks to the wisdom that comes from spending daily time in the Word, all that resulted was some embarrassment and hopefully some conviction for the distracted driver, and, of course, a very grateful mom and her 4 children. Experiences like this have happened to my family and I more times than I can count, and I am so very grateful for the Word of God that has been planted in my heart, and the wisdom, protection and guidance it provides for my family and me.

My prayer for you is that you, too, will crave the Word in such a way that you cannot bear to start your days without filling up on the Word. With this intimate knowledge of His Word, you will find that hearing His voice is as clear as hearing the birds on a warm, sunny day, or hearing the voices of your family as they bustle through the house. Your spirit and the Spirit of the Lord will become best friends.

5. Praying in the Will of God

In order for us to have the most success with our prayers, we must know and understand what God's will is - for ourselves, and for those we are praying for. A big promise comes from knowing and praying in the Lord's will, and that promise is shown to us in the book of First John:

*This is the confidence we have in approaching God: that if we ask anything according to His will, He hears us. And if we know that He hears us - whatever we ask - we **know** that we have what we asked of Him.* (1 John 5:14-15)

What a wonderful promise! What an awesome God we serve - One who is willing to give us whatever we ask if it is in His will!

So, why is being in His will with our prayers so important? Remember that because the Enemy still roams to and fro on the earth, seeking whom he may devour (1 Peter 5:8), we as humans are still in danger of being influenced by evil, or of hearing the Enemy's voice instead of God's when a prompting to pray comes on our hearts. Can you imagine the trouble we could cause if the Lord simply agreed to answer all of our prayers? Once something is done, it's done. A re-do is not an option.

When a person first accepts Christ as their Lord and Savior, knowing and growing in the Lord's will and in the knowledge of His commands on how we are to live is a process. Very rarely does one come into the knowledge of the Word without spending countless hours in the reading of the Word and in prayer. If you are saved, I'm certain most all of you can look back at your walk in Christ and see where you may have, in the beginning, held certain beliefs about how Christians were to behave, or how the rest of the world was to behave. With 99% of us, these beliefs have evolved and changed over time as the Lord and His Word have shown us how to stop living our way and start living His way. I know this is the case in my life. As a new Christian, I was so focused on getting people saved that I was convinced I had to tell them how to live - to tell them the difference between right and wrong and about how God called them to live - whether they wanted to hear it or not. I also see now that I had quite a bit of pride about being a Christian. My conversations with God were very self-focused, and not very God-focused, and my others-focused prayers revolved around wanting *them* to behave better, like me! If my prayers would have all been answered back then, I may have brought some people to Christ, but boy, I'm not sure at all that they would've been walking the glorious path the Lord has hand-picked for them.

Praise the Lord, however, He promises that He will grant us the requests we pray that are in *His* will, and not ours! When we are submissive enough to allow the Lord to train and refine our hearts, we will be better able to see and understand His will, and pray correctly.

So what exactly is God's will? Let's go to the Word and find out.

Praying in Love

We must always keep in mind when discerning God's will that *God is love* (1 John 4:16). This is your first clue that will tell you whether what you are asking of God in prayer is right or wrong. If your prayer isn't out of love - if it is a prayer said in anger or vengeance, or for someone to "learn their lesson", you're on the wrong path. Yes, God is a God of correction and rebuke, but Romans 14:4 warns us sternly *"Who are you to judge another man's servant? To his own master he stands or falls. And he will stand, for the Lord is able to make him stand."* And Romans 12:19 promises *"Vengeance is mine; I will repay." Saith the Lord.*

The reason the Lord asks us to leave judgment and vengeance on His plate is because only God truly knows the heart of each man or woman. Look back at the sins you've committed - the mistakes you've made. Isn't it fair to say that the things you've done wrong were unintentional, or done out of pain? People rarely mean to hurt one another, and if they do intend to, it's usually out of intense pain or sadness. Their hearts, at the core, are good, but when we are thrown, by the Enemy, a life of pain, abandonment and loneliness, sometimes we just don't know what else to do but act out as a cry for attention. Or sometimes when we see others being wronged by an act that once caused pain in our lives, the memories of that hurt and seeing another wronged in that same way is so painful that we react toward another's similar situation in pain and anger. This is wrong, of course, but our hearts are still good. We just don't want to see anyone else go through the same pain that we went through earlier in our lives. So, let's leave judging and revenge on God's plate, where it belongs. This one decision alone can reduce the stress in your life dramatically.

Another important factor in walking in love and praying in love is to know that it is God's will that all be saved. Let's look at the book of First Timothy:

I urge, then, first of all, that requests, prayers, intercession and thanksgiving be made for **everyone** *- for kings and all those in authority, that we may live peaceful and quiet lives in all godliness and holiness.* ***This is good, and pleases God our Savior, who wants all men to be saved and to come to a knowledge of the truth.*** (1 Timothy 2:3-4)

5. Praying in the Will of God

God's love for mankind is so great that, regardless of the magnitude of the sins someone has committed, it is always His deepest desire that they repent and run to Him for the restoration and cleansing power of the Blood of Jesus Christ. In fact, by far, the most prevailing theme throughout the entire New Testament is love - God's love for us, and His plea for us to love one another as He loves us. This command of love comes with many promises of blessings if we obey it and many promises of trouble if we don't. It also shows us that when we are not walking in love with someone that it's *our* problem, and not the problem of the person with whom we are angry. Let's go again to the Word:

*This is the message you have heard from the beginning: We should **love** one another. Do not be like Cain, who belonged to the evil one and murdered his brother. And why did he murder him? **Because his own actions were evil and his brother's were righteous.** Anyone who hates his brother is a murderer, and you know that no murderer has eternal life in him. **This is how we know what love is; Jesus Christ laid down His life for us. And we ought to lay down our lives for our brothers.** If anyone has material possessions and sees his brother in need but has no pity on him, how can the love of God be in him? Dear children, let us not love with words or tongue but with actions and in truth.* (1 John 3:11, 12, 15-18)

And more from the disciple John:

Dear friends, let us love one another, for love comes from God. Everyone who loves has been born of God and knows God. Whoever does not love does not know God, because

God is love. *If anyone says, "I love God," yet hates his brother, he is a liar. For anyone who does not love his brother, whom he has seen, cannot love God, whom he has not seen. And He has given us this command: <u>Whoever loves God must also love his brother.</u>* (1 John 4: 7-8, 20-21)

The book of Matthew tells us that loving our brother requires loving ALL people.

<u>*But I tell you: Love your enemies and pray for those who persecute you, that you may be sons of your Father in heaven… If you love those who love you, what reward will you get? Are not even the tax collectors doing that? And if you greet only your brothers, what are you doing more than others? Do not even pagans do that? Be perfect, therefore, as your heavenly Father is perfect.*</u> (Matthew 5:44-48)

The book of Romans tells us to:

Let no debt remain outstanding, except the continuing debt to love one another, for he who loves his fellow man has fulfilled the law. (Romans 13:8)

And the book of First Corinthians, one of the most famous books in the Bible about love, tells us:

If I speak in the tongues of men and of angels, but have not love, I am only a resounding gong or a clanging cymbal. If I have the gift of prophecy and can fathom all mysteries and all knowledge, and if I have a faith that can move mountains, but have not love, I am nothing. If I give all I possess to the poor and surrender my body to the flames, but have not love,

5. Praying in the Will of God

I gain nothing. Love is patient, love is kind. It does not envy, it does not boast, it is not proud. It is not rude, it is not self-seeking, it is not easily angered, it keeps no record of wrongs. Love does not delight in evil, but rejoices with the truth. It always protects, always trusts, always hopes, always perseveres. Love never fails. (1 Corinthians. 13:1-8)

The Bible is very clear, too, about those who do not walk in love and their salvation, or lack of it:

This is how we know who the children of God are and who the children of the devil are: Anyone who does not do what is right is not a child of God: nor is anyone who does not love his brother (1 John 3:10)

I realize that it's very hard to walk in love with someone who has caused great harm to you or those you love. It feels like because the offender doesn't deserve that love that we shouldn't give it to them, but that's not what the Word of God instructs us to do. The Word says *love*. End of conversation. If you are having a hard time walking in love with someone who has hurt you, ask the Lord to help you see that person the way He sees them, and make a choice today to walk in love with that person. This doesn't mean you have to see them or take their abuse. Part of respecting your body and your mind, which God says are the temple of the Holy Spirit, is to keep it safe from those who would do you harm. So even if you must choose to stay away from those who continue to cause you harm, walk in love with them anyway. It will heal your heart, and it just may soften that other person's hard-heartedness, causing them to come to repentance of their own.

I want to stop here and address a great controversy in the body of Christ - the issue of sin and the unsaved, or, the saved for that matter. We've all experienced watching people who are blatantly living in sin of some sort or another living "Godly", active lives in the church, and ignoring their sin, or, worse yet, claiming their sins are acceptable to God. As frustrating as this can be for people, and as worried as they are about God's reputation and the church's reputation, we must always keep in mind that we are to:

1. Love our "enemies".
2. Not judge another man's servant.

God is perfectly capable of protecting His reputation and clearing His Name, although He has no need to, because He IS righteousness and truth. And don't forget the fact that *"all have sinned and fallen short of the glory of God."* (Romans 3:23).

If you are truly walking in love, as God calls us to, the very best way that you can advance God's Name and His cause is to love that sinning brother or sister with all of your heart, and pray fervently for them to have God's wisdom and knowledge and truth come full board into their hearts. This is not to say that you should condone sin of any kind - we should never condone sin. In fact, part of truly walking in love with others is to stand up against their sinfulness – *when the Lord leads you to.* If you're calling someone out on their sin of your own accord, it won't be successful, but more than likely it will be offensive, causing that person to stand even firmer in their sin. Pray and wait for God's leading before "speaking the truth in love" (Ephesians 4:15) about someone else's sin. We need to realize that in a situation like this, praying in love is the most powerful weapon we have.

When the body of Christ comes to understand that it is through strife and hate that the Enemy gains ground, and learns to use the very powerful weapon of loving prayer to defeat him, people will be accepting Christ so fast that we'll be building churches on every corner. Make a decision today to obey God's call on us to walk in love - completely. Not only will it change your life, it will change the lives of everyone around you.

Praying in Faith

Praying in faith is another very powerful weapon we have when it comes to seeing our prayers answered. Let's look and see what the Word has to say about faith and how it affects our prayers. We'll start by going again to Mark Chapter 11:

"Have faith in God," Jesus answered. <u>"For assuredly I say to you, whoever says to this mountain, 'Be removed and be cast into the sea,' and does not doubt in his heart, but believes that those things he says will be done, he will have whatever he says. Therefore I say to you, whatever things you ask when you pray, believe that you receive them, and you will have them."</u> (Mark 11:22-24)

This is a very powerful statement, made by the Lord Jesus Christ Himself. Webster's Dictionary describes faith, in part, as "trust or confidence; belief in the statement of another, belief in the truth of revealed religion; **confidence and trust in God**. The Bible, however, has its own definition of faith:

Faith is the substance of things hoped for, the evidence of things not seen. (Hebrews 11:1).

Do you trust God? I mean *really* trust Him? Trusting God involves not only believing that what He says in His Word is true, but it also involves believing what God says is true **for you.** The Lord dealt with me on this issue ever so clearly one day when I was condemning myself for a sin I had committed long ago. I was sitting in the dark in the parking lot of the church we attended at the time. I had gone one night to meet with friends to pray. After we prayed, I walked in the dark to my car, and as I got in the car, the Enemy started to push guilt and condemnation in my mind over this particular sin. "*I forgive you,*" the Lord reminded me. "*But Lord,*" I reminded Him, *"that was a terrible thing I did!"* The Lord said to me *"Are you saying that my Beloved Son's death and resurrection on the cross isn't good enough to wipe out this sin?"*

I was speechless. I had never thought about it that way before, and when the Lord put it in that perspective, I could only humbly repent, and I made a decision right then and there that I would not disrespect Jesus' sacrifice for me in that way ever again.

One area where I see the Body of Christ really missing out on all that God has for them is this area. We see His promises in the Word. We believe that they are true, but we believe that they are true for *others,* not for us personally. This comes from just not having a clear enough vision about who we are in Christ.

Remember that we learned in Chapter 2 that we are:

"heirs of God and co-heirs with Christ..."(Romans Chapter 8)

and that God also promises:

<u>**I will be a Father to you, and you will be my sons and daughters.**</u> (2 Corinthians Chapter 6. Also in Lev. 26:12, Ez. 37:27 and Jer. 32:38)

This is a revelation we must get deep into our Spirits and our minds if we are to have faith-filled prayers. As co-heirs with Christ, God sees us, through Jesus, as His very own children! Remember that Jesus, our Big Brother, says that:

<u>"I tell you the truth**, anyone who has faith in Me** will do what I have been doing. He will do even greater things that these, because I am going to the Father. And I will do whatever you ask in my name, so that the Son may bring glory to the Father. You may ask me for anything in My Name, and I will do it."</u> (John 14:12-14)

Jesus is our Defender. It is through the shedding of His Blood on the cross that we are allowed to be adopted, by God, as His own sons and daughters! Therefore, God sees us through the perfection of His Son, Jesus - with rose-colored glasses, so to speak. Our sins and imperfections have been eliminated on the cross - they no longer exist, and since the Creator of the universe has said this is so, have we any authority to argue that fact? Absolutely not! On the contrary, let's praise Him and rejoice and shout "Hallelujah!" for we are free!

Another thing we need to know about faith is that it involves believing what the Word says, even though the circumstances around you may look completely different. Remember that Hebrews 11:1 says: *"Faith is the substance of things hoped for, the evidence of things not seen."* **A strong faith will allow you to know that when you pray for something that is in the will of God, you can be sure it will be done, even when the circumstances around you and the physical evidence you see look contrary.**

This goes hand in hand with the Book of Matthew when Jesus says *"I tell you the truth, if you have faith and do not doubt, not only can you do what was done to the fig tree* (that we learned about earlier), *but also you can say to this mountain, 'Go, throw yourself into the sea,' and it will be done for you.* **If you believe, you will receive whatever you ask for in prayer.** (Matthew 21:21-22). Yet, keep in mind that this still comes with the stipulation that we are asking what is in God's will, according to 1 John chapter 5.

Now let's look at what else the Word has to say about faith. Faith, it's clear, is the tool that gets things done in the Kingdom.

5. Praying in the Will of God

It is a tool that heals:

*Just then, a woman who had been subject to bleeding for twelve years came up behind Him and touched the edge of His cloak. For she had said to herself, "If only I may touch His garment, I will be made well." Jesus turned to her and saw her. <u>"Be of good cheer, daughter,"</u> he said, **"your faith has made you well."** And the woman was healed from that very moment.* (Matthew 9:20-22)

*As Jesus went on from there, two blind men followed Him, calling out, "Have mercy on us, Son of David!" When He had gone indoors, the blind men came to Him and He asked them, <u>"Do you believe that I am able to do this?"</u> "Yes, Lord," they replied. Then He touched their eyes and said, **<u>"According to your faith it will be done to you"</u>**, and their sight was restored.* (Matthew 9:27-30).

*In Lystra, there sat a man crippled in his feet, who was lame from birth and had never walked. He listened to Paul as he was speaking. Paul, observing him intently and **seeing that he had faith to be healed**, said with a loud voice, "Stand up on your feet!" And he leaped up and walked.* (Acts 14:8-10)

It is a tool that strengthens:

<u>*Consider how the lilies grow. They do not labor or spin. Yet I tell you, not even Solomon in all his splendor was dressed like one of these. If that is how God clothes the grass of the field, which is here today, and tomorrow is thrown into the fire, how much more will he clothe you, O you of little faith!"*</u> (Luke 12:27-28)

Be on your guard; stand firm in the faith; be men of courage; be strong. (1 Corinthians 16:13)

Believe in the Lord your God and you will be established; have faith in His prophets and you shall prosper. (2 Chronicles 20:20)

It is a tool that saves:

For it in the righteousness of God is revealed from faith to faith; as it is written, "<u>The just shall live by faith</u>." (Romans 1:17, quoting Habakkuk 2:4)

This righteousness from God comes through faith in Jesus Christ to all who believe. (Romans 3:22)

Therefore, since we have been justified by faith, we have peace with God through our Lord Jesus Christ, through whom we have gained access by faith into this grace in which we now stand. (Romans 5:1-2)

So what are the downfalls of praying prayers without faith to back them up? Several potential dangers lie in wait for those whose faith is lacking or who are struggling with unbelief (the sister to a lack of faith).

Prayers without faith lack power:

Then the disciples came to Jesus in private and asked, "Why couldn't we drive the demon out?" Jesus replied, "<u>Because of your unbelief. I tell you the truth, if you have faith as small as a mustard seed, you can say to this mountain,</u>

'Move from here to there' and it will move. Nothing will be impossible for you. (Matthew 17:19-21)

Prayers without faith displease God:

A man in the crowd answered, "Teacher, I brought you my son, who is possessed by a spirit that has robbed him of speech. Whenever it seizes him, it throws him to the ground. He foams at the mouth, gnashes his teeth and becomes rigid. I asked your disciples to drive out the spirit, but they could not. "O, unbelieving generation," Jesus replied, "how long shall I stay with you? How long must I put up with you? Bring the boy to me." (Mark 9:17-19).

In fact, the Word says that: *without faith it is impossible to please God, for he who comes to God must believe that He is, and that He is a rewarder of those who diligently seek Him.* (Hebrews 11:6)

Prayers without faith are considered sinful:

*But the man who has doubts is condemned if he eats, because he does not eat from faith, for whatever **does not come from faith is sin**.* (Romans 14:23)

A lack of faith can even jeopardize our walk with Him:

"At that time, many will turn away from the faith and will betray and hate each other, and many false prophets will appear and deceive many people. Because of the increase of wickedness, the love of most will grow cold,

but he who stands firm to the end will be saved. (Matthew 24:10-13)

Faith is so important to God, and so powerful, that it can even make a way for you where none may have been before! Let's look again at the Book of Matthew:

Leaving that place, Jesus withdrew to the region of Tyre and Sidon. A Canaanite woman from that vicinity came to Him, crying out, "Lord, Son of David, have mercy on me! My daughter is severely demon-possessed. Jesus did not answer a word. So His disciples came to him and urged him, "Send her away, for she keeps crying out after us." Jesus then answered her "I was sent only to the lost sheep of Israel." The woman came and knelt before him. "Lord, help me!" she said. Jesus replied, "It is not right to take the children's bread and toss it to their dogs." "Yes Lord," the woman replied, "but even the dogs eat the crumbs that fall from their masters' table." Then Jesus answered, "Woman, you have great faith! Your request is granted." And her daughter was healed from that very hour. (Matthew 15:21-28)

This woman's prayer was answered because she knew, without a doubt, that Jesus is the Great Healer, and she wasn't about to give up on her prayers until she got the answer that she knew was God's will - that by His stripes, we are healed! You see, regardless of our faith - or lack thereof - God is forever faithful.

In Romans 3:3 we learn *What if some did not have faith? Will their lack of faith nullify God's faithfulness? Not at all! Let God be true and every man a liar.*

5. Praying in the Will of God

God is faithful - through and through. Regardless of where our walk is, and at what level our faith is, God remains steadfast and completely faithful to the promises in His Word. We, however, need to know and *believe* in God's faithfulness with all of our hearts if we want to see our prayers answered consistently. So let's work at increasing our faith to believe that what He says is true!

How do we do that? Simply by making a commitment to reading and studying the Word as a part of our obedience in seeking first the Kingdom of God and His righteousness. (Matthew 6:33)

Romans 10:17 says that *Faith comes by hearing, and hearing by the Word of God.* Reading and studying the Word of God is the only way to increase your faith, so make a commitment to study the Word relentlessly and increase your faith - today and always.

A note about the "Name it and Claim it" religions: I'm sure all of you have at least heard of the "Name it and Claim it" preachers. I'm here to tell you that there is a big difference between the Name it and Claim it teachings, and the Faith teachings. Both may focus on God's goodness, but true Faith teachers know and teach that although God wants to bless us simply because He loves us, that His primary reason for wanting people to have healing, prosperity, protection and other blessings is so that we have the means to share the Gospel and show the love of Christ to others. False faith teachers put the focus on *you* and what you can *get* from God for yourself. There is an easy way to tell the difference between the two: First, listen to the teaching and see whom the focus is on, and second, check their Bible quotes. If they're taking verses out of context, or leaving crucial before and after verses out of their verse focus, something's wrong.

God is indeed a good God. He loves us and wants to bless us - that's why Jesus was sent to redeem us from the curse (see Galatians 3:13-14). In order to walk in God's best blessings, however, we must believe that He loves us and *wants* to bless us, and, more importantly, we must *"seek first the Kingdom of God and His righteousness"*. God's main purpose for us on this earth is to bring people into the kingdom of God by sharing the love of Jesus Christ and the Gospel Message with them. Let's focus on His task for us, and gain the faith to believe that *"my God will meet all your needs according the His glorious riches in Christ Jesus."* (Philippians 4:19). Give the Lord the chance to show you who He really is!

Praying with an Earnest Heart

If you are expecting God to hear and answer your prayers, you must be willing to come to Him with an earnest and committed heart. Your words must be spoken not simply for the purpose of speaking them, but as a heartfelt desire to be closer to God and to assist in accomplishing His purposes on this earth. In the book of Matthew, God speaks of this:

"And when you pray, do not be like the hypocrites, for they love to pray standing in the synagogues and on the street corners to be seen by men. I tell you the truth; they have

5. Praying in the Will of God

received their reward in full. But when you pray, go into your room, close the door, and pray to your Father, who is unseen. Then your Father, who sees what is done in secret, will reward you. And when you pray, do not use vain repetitions like the heathen do, for they think they will be heard because of their many words. Therefore, do not be like them. For your Father knows what you need before you ask him. This, then, is how you should pray:

Our Father, who art in Heaven, hallowed be thy name.

Thy kingdom come, thy will be done, on earth as it is in heaven.

Give us this day our daily bread, and forgive us our sins, as we forgive those who sin against us.

And lead us not into temptation, but deliver us from the evil one, for Yours is the kingdom and the power and the glory forever. Amen. (Matthew 6:5-13)

There are a few things we can learn from this passage. Number one, the hypocrites and the heathens displeased the Lord with their prayers because their prayers were not from their hearts. The hypocrites were praying simply to be heard praying and gain attention to their self-perceived godliness. The heathens were simply harassing the Lord, babbling endlessly without sincerity. Prayers offered up in these ways will only close God's ears to the requestor.

Secondly, there are key points offered up in the Lord's Prayer that make it worthy of His attention:

1. It starts by praising the Lord and acknowledging His authority.
2. It asks that *His* will be done
3. It acknowledges that we need Him (*give us our daily bread, deliver us from evil*)
4. It acknowledges that we need to do our part and have right hearts (*forgive us our sins, as we forgive those who sin against us*)

Effective prayers come with an earnest heart and should have the 4 qualities listed above. Humility is key. Yes, God has given us authority over all the earth, but He is still God, and He is still our Master, and so we must acknowledge Him with the respect that we should have for a Father. Just as a father here on earth has a much more open heart to an obedient child than a disobedient one, our Father in heaven longs to hear and answers the prayers of His children who love Him, respect Him and seek Him first.

Walking in Obedience

Living a life obedient to God's commands is another very important aspect when it comes to praying in the will of God. Now, God has made it clear that we who have accepted Jesus' coming, His death, and His resurrection as payment for our sin are blemish-free in His sight. Praise God, He looks at us through His Son, and sees our sin no more:

So Christ was sacrificed once to take away the sins of many people; (Hebrews 9:28)

5. Praying in the Will of God

This does not mean, however, that those who have accepted Jesus in their hearts may go on freely, living in the same sin they did before accepting Jesus. In fact, the Word makes it quite clear that those who choose to continue living sinful lives really are not saved at all. Let's look at some of those compelling verses:

Whoever abides in Him does not sin. Whoever sins has neither seen Him nor known Him. Little children, let no one deceive you. He who practices righteousness is righteous, just as He is righteous. He who sins is of the devil, for the devil has sinned from the beginning. For this purpose the Son of God was manifested, that He might destroy the works of the devil. Whoever has been born of God does not sin, for His seed remains in him, and he cannot sin, because he has been born of God. (1 John 3:6-9).

*We know that anyone born of God **does not continue to sin;** the One who was born of God keeps him safe, and the evil one cannot harm him.* (1 John 5:18)

Likewise you also, reckon yourselves to be dead indeed to sin, but alive to God in Christ Jesus our Lord. (Romans 6:11)

…let us throw off everything that hinders and the sin that so easily entangles, and let us run with perseverance the race marked out for us. (Hebrews 12:1)

Now, we have to address God's grace here, because that is indeed what saves those who believe from the pits of Hell. Jesus came to "take away the sins of the world", meaning that in God's sight they exist no more, and that our foul-ups after receiving Christ as our Lord and Savior are still forgiven - covered by grace. Indeed, Romans 5:20 says, *"where sin increased, grace increased all the more."*

But let's look at Romans Chapter 6:

What shall we say, then? Shall we continue in sin that grace may abound? Certainly not! How shall we who died to sin live any longer in it? Or do you not know that as many of us as were baptized into Christ Jesus were baptized into His death? Therefore we were buried with Him through baptism into death, that just as Christ was raised from the dead by the glory of the Father, even so we also should walk in the newness of life.

For if we have been united together in the likeness of His death, certainly we also shall be in the likeness of His resurrection, knowing this, that our old man was crucified with Him, that the body of sin might be done away with, that we should no longer be slaves of sin. For he who has died has been freed from sin. Now if we died with Christ, we believe that we shall also live with Him, knowing that Christ, having been raised from the dead, dies no more. Death no longer has dominion over Him. For the death that He died, He died to sin once for all; but the life that He lives, He lives to God. Likewise you also, reckon yourselves to be dead indeed to sin, but alive to God in Christ Jesus our Lord. **Therefore do not let sin reign in your mortal body, that you should obey it in its lusts**. *And do not present your members as instruments of unrighteousness to sin, but present yourselves to God as being alive from the dead, and your members as instruments of righteousness to God. For sin shall not have dominion over* *you, for you are not under law but under grace. What then? Shall we sin because we are not under law but under grace? Certainly not! Do you not know that to whom you present yourselves slaves to obey, you are that one's slaves whom you obey, whether of sin leading to death, or of obedience leading to righteousness? But God be thanked that though you were slaves of sin, yet you obeyed from the heart that form of doctrine to which you were delivered. And having been set free from sin, you became slaves of righteousness.* (Romans 6:1-18).

So, how does this work then, God's grace? How can our sins continue to be covered by grace, yet the Word also commands us to sin no more and tells us that if we do, we're in trouble?

The issue is simply one of the heart. Grace was not given us in order that we may go on living in sin, knowing that we're "covered". Grace was given us knowing that, until the day of the Second Coming, we are still subject to weakness and error. It is our duty, however, to do our very best to *"seek first the kingdom of God and His righteousness."* And those who are saved will truly desire right living. It is out of honor for God that we should be working, daily, toward a life that is more and more void of sin, and more and more immersed in righteousness. Soak the Word into your heart every day and learn how God expects you to walk, talk and behave. Make a commitment to seek and follow His desires for your behavior, for God will indeed check our hearts. The heart that ignores its sin, and expects a free ride on God's grace, however, should heed the warning in the Book of Matthew:

*"Not everyone who says to me 'Lord, Lord' will enter the kingdom of heaven, **but only he who does the will of my Father who is in heaven.** Many will say to me on that day, 'Lord, Lord, did we not prophesy in you name, and in your name drive out demons and perform many miracles?' Then I will tell them plainly, 'I never knew you. Away from me, you evildoers!'* (Matthew 7:21-23)

And the book of James tells us:

But be doers of the Word, and not hearers only, deceiving yourselves. For if anyone is a hearer of the Word and not a doer, he is like a man observing his natural face in a mirror; for he observes himself, goes away, and immediately forgets what kind of man he was. (James 1:22-24)

The heart that truly strives for a sin-free life and truly *seeks first the kingdom of God and His righteousness*, that is the heart that will receive God's mercy and grace and have God hear their prayers. A walk pleasing to God requires frequent check-ups. Check your actions daily, and see whether or not they line up with the Word of God and its commands about how we are to live. If not, I plead with you to get in line with His will, so that you will indeed take your seat at the Feast with Abraham, Isaac and Jacob.

It's important, too, to remember that the only way to truly know His will is to know His Word. Study it and make it your life's work. Pray for a desire to crave the Word. Ask the Lord, fervently, to give you wisdom, for God says that *"If any of you lacks wisdom, he should ask God, who gives to*

5. Praying in the Will of God

all liberally and without reproach, and it will be given to him." (James 1:5)

The promises that come with having wisdom are far from just pleasing the Lord, although that should be the only reason we need. Proverbs Chapter 3 tells us:

Happy is the man who finds wisdom, the man who gains understanding, for she is more profitable that silver, and yields better returns than gold. She is more precious than rubies; nothing you desire can compare with her. Long life is in her right hand; in her left hand are riches and honor. Her ways are ways of pleasantness, and all of her paths are peace. She is a tree of life to those who embrace her; those who lay hold of her will be blessed. (Proverbs 3: 13:18)

Walking in obedience to the Lord, and walking in His Wisdom, will only keep you on God's path, keep you off of the Devil's path, and therefore increase the magnitude and success of your prayers. You see, the more we are one with Him in spirit, the more unified we are with God and His will, the more He is able to answer our prayers. See God's promise below in the book of First John:

Beloved, if our heart does not condemn us (of our wrongdoing), *we have confidence toward God. And whatever we ask we receive from Him, because we keep His commandments and do those things that are pleasing in His sight. And this is His commandment: that we should believe on the name of His Son Jesus Christ and love one another, as He gave us commandment.* (1 John 3:21-23)

And let's look again in the book of Psalms:

Come and listen, all you who fear God; let me tell you what He has done for me. I cried out to Him with my mouth; His praise was on my tongue. **If I had cherished sin in my heart, the Lord would not have listened. But God has surely listened and heard my voice in prayer.** *Praise be to God, who has not rejected my prayer or withheld His love from me!* (Psalm 66:16-20)

Remember: sin always, always separates us from God, and aligns us with the Devil, because to sin is to choose the Devil's side. Christian or not, you cannot willingly walk in the ways of the Devil, choosing to live a life of sinfulness, and expect to be in unity with God. That's like expecting to live life with a healthy, strong body, and eating cheeseburgers and fries at every meal - it just doesn't work! So, get in line with the Word of God and with the will of God, and watch your lives be transformed, *that you may prove what is the good and acceptable and perfect will of God.* (Romans 12:2)

Walking in obedience also means that we choose to *trust* God. First Chronicles 5:20 shows us this:

They were helped in fighting (their enemies), and God handed the Hagrites and all their allies over to them, because they cried out to Him during the battle. He answered their prayers, **because they trusted in Him.**

Choose today to trust that God is what His Word says He is, even above the circumstances that you see in your life. Making that choice will not only increase your faith, it will also help you to see God in a whole new light, and change your life for the better all the way around.

Praying in the Spirit

I want to address praying in the Spirit, or praying in tongues, for just a moment here. The Bible speaks clearly in several places about the gift of praying in tongues. I know that there are churches out there that believe that the gift of tongues, along with the other gifts of the Spirit, were for the early church only. I can find no evidence of this in the Word. In fact, the Book of First Corinthians says clearly *"Therefore my brothers, be eager to prophesy, and do not forbid speaking in tongues. But everything should be done in a fitting and orderly way."* (1 Corinthians 14:39).

In the book of Mark, Jesus appeared after the resurrection and came to the disciples, saying <u>*"Go into all the world and preach the Gospel to every creature. He who believes and is baptized will be saved; but he who does not believe will be condemned. And these signs will follow those who believe: in My name they will cast out demons; they will speak with new tongues; they will take up serpents; and if they drink anything deadly it will by no means hurt them; they will lay the hands on the sick, and they will recover.*</u> (Mark 16:15-18)

What exactly is praying in tongues? Praying in tongues is simply a gift of the Spirit that allows our spirit to have a more direct line of communication with the Holy Spirit.

First Corinthians chapter 14 says that, *"anyone who speaks in a tongue does not speak to men, but to God. Indeed, no one understands him; he utters mysteries with his spirit."* (1 Corinthians 14:2).

Speaking in tongues is done through our spirit, which has a much clearer view of the Lord than our minds do. Think of it this way: The teacher at school knows your child. They teach him every day. They know how well he does at math, reading, etc., and they know how he interacts with the other students. But you, as his parent, know *why* he does what he does. You know intimately what he does when he's hurt, scared, happy or sad. You know that if he goes to bed a half- hour late, you'll be in for trouble the next day. Or if he eats too much dairy, he'll be spending some time in the bathroom. The teacher may know that your son is crabby, but he won't know *why* he's crabby. In the same way, our spirits know God better than our minds do, because our minds often get cluttered with the cares of this world.

The gift of speaking in tongues allows our spirits to talk with God, praise God, and pray to God in a way that's more aligned with His will. Baptism of the Holy Spirit, which ushers in the gift of speaking in tongues, is available to all believers who are willing to ask for it. If you don't come from a church that teaches about the gifts of the Spirit, this can be uncomfortable and maybe a bit scary at first. So simply go to the Lord with your fears, and find a trustworthy pastor or friend who understands the gifts of the spirit, and God will show you the way.

5. Praying in the Will of God

Knowing His Will

So, when it comes to specific prayers, how do we know that what we are asking for is lining up with His will? Well, sometimes we do, and sometimes we don't. Our first task is to go to the Word. If what you are asking for lines up with His Word, you're on the right track. This is simple when you are praying for someone's salvation, or for reconciliation of a broken relationship, or for healing. We know these things are all in God's will, because the Bible says they're in God's will. But what about prayers directly related to our lives, like, where we should work, where we should live, who we should marry - things like that?

Three of the key elements that have helped our family tremendously in areas like this are:

1. Ask the Lord, consistently, to shape the desires of your heart, or the heart of whoever you're praying for, so that they line up with the desires of His heart for you, your family, or whatever His desire is about the particular situation you're praying for.
2. Ask the Lord for wisdom, discernment and knowledge, regarding the specific situation and regarding life in general.
3. Learn to recognize God's still, small voice. The more time you spend in prayer, and the more time you spend in the Word, the easier it will be for you to know whether the instructions and information you are hearing in your spirit are from God or from the Enemy.

Also, remember this: The Enemy can hear your voice when you are praying, but he can only guess at your thoughts when you're praying. I pray in silence - just my spirit speaking to the Lord, at all times, with the exception of:

-When I'm praying with others

-When my prayers involve reminding the Enemy that I know full well what the Word says about a situation, and that I am standing on the Word for that particular situation

-When I'm praising the Lord

It's important for us to remember that as Christians, although Jesus has won the war for us, we still have an Enemy fighting to deceive us. We are soldiers for Christ, fighting a very important battle, and we must know full well who our Enemy is and what His tactics are. Then and only then will we have the power and knowledge to defeat him.

Know Your Enemy

It's easy when things are so crazy in the world to think that it is the people that our fight is with. After all, it's the people who do the terrible things in this world, right? It's the people who hurt us, isn't it? We need to remember, however, that the sin in this world comes not directly from the people, but from the deception the Enemy, Satan, is using to fool people into doing things to harm others; things that are outside of God's will.

The book of Ephesians makes this very clear:

Finally, be strong in the Lord and in His mighty power. Put on the full armor of God so that you can take your stand against the wiles of the Devil. **For we do not wrestle against flesh and blood,** *but against principalities, against powers, against the rulers of the darkness of this age, against spiritual hosts of wickedness in the heavenly places.* (Ephesians 6:10-12)

When Paul talks here about principalities and powers, he's talking not about people, but about the Devil and his helpers. *Remember:* when Adam chose to obey Satan in the garden, he gave his God-given dominion over the earth to Satan. Now, Jesus purchased that authority back for us when He died on the cross and rose again, but because so many on earth are unaware of that, they still let the Devil run rampant. **The only power the Devil has left is the power of deception,** and he uses that power to deceive others into doing ungodly things, into walking off of God's path, and to trick people into believing that his works are God's will. In reality, though, if we only knew the Word better, and knew that God has given us authority over all the power of the Enemy (Luke 10:19), we wouldn't let him get away with nearly as much as he gets away with! Satan is no more than a neighborhood bully, trying to mess with kids and instill fear in them, but we, as Christians, have a Daddy who is much bigger and stronger than any bully. He's a Daddy who is ready and waiting for us to realize that He has given us, through Jesus and His shed blood, the strength to kick that bully to the curb!

Search the Word intensely, and *taste and see that the Lord is good.* (Psalm 34:8). You'll soon learn to know well the difference between the Lord's will and the Enemy's lies.

Praise and Give Thanks to the Lord

Praising the Lord and giving thanks to Him is another key factor in seeing prayers work. The Bible is full – *full* - of verses that instruct us to praise and give thanks to the Lord. Here are just a few:

I will proclaim the Name of the Lord. Oh praise the greatness of our God! (Deuteronomy 32:3)

The Lord is my strength and my song; He has become my salvation. He is my God, and I will praise Him, my father's God, and I will exalt Him. (Exodus 15:2)

For the Lord is great and greatly to be praised; (1 Chronicles 16:25)

Praise to the Lord, for His mercy endures forever. (2 Chronicles 20:21)

Rejoice in the Lord, O you righteous (remember; you are righteous in God's sight!); *for praise from the upright is beautiful. Praise the Lord with the harp; make music to Him on the ten-stringed lyre. Sing to Him a new song; play skillfully, and shout for joy.* (Psalm 33: 1-3)

5. Praying in the Will of God

Do not be anxious about anything, but in everything, by prayer and petition, with thanksgiving, let your requests be made known to God. (Philippians 4:6)

Praising the Lord and giving thanks to Him are very powerful weapons in your spiritual arsenal, because it ushers us into God's presence - into His throne room, where God is magnified and the Enemy is not allowed to come. Praise and thanksgiving also please the Lord immensely. All prayer sessions, no matter how big or small, should be started with praise and thanksgiving to the Lord. Even in the darkest of circumstances, finding what you can praise the Lord about will help usher you out of darkness. Praise Him for your home, your food, your family, and your life. Praise Him for the grass, and the trees. Praise Him for the one working part on your body if that's all that works. Just get into place where the **focus is off of your circumstances and onto the Lord**. Prayer sessions should also end with praise and thanksgiving as well. Remember that the book of Mark says that we are to *"believe you receive them when we ask".* Thanking and praising the Lord for answering our prayers is a faith action step that solidifies the fact that we have chosen to believe that we have received – in the spiritual realm - what we have asked of the Lord, if we are asking with a correct heart and within His will. Use these weapons of praise and thanksgiving to defeat the Enemy and to move the mountains in your life regularly!

6. Breaking Down Roadblocks

Let's talk now about those unanswered prayers, and what some of the causes could be. Since we know God loves us and wants the best for us, what are the reasons some of our prayers seem to go unanswered? This was a question that I really struggled with, so I asked the Lord for wisdom in this area. Here are some of the areas that He showed me that can be roadblocks in our prayer life.

Sin

Most all roadblocks to our prayers result from sin of one kind or another. This can be our own sin, or the sin of those we've been praying for, but the Bible makes it clear that our obedience to Him and His Word has a definite connection to our answered prayers. Let's look at the book of Second Chronicles:

<u>"If My people, who are called by My Name, will humble themselves and pray and seek My face**, and turn from their wicked ways**, then will I hear from Heaven and will forgive their sin and will heal their land. Now my eyes will be open and my ears attentive to the prayers offered in this place.</u> (2 Chronicles 7:14-15)

Again, too, in the book of John, Jesus makes a connection between us hearing the Lord and our obedience:

<u>"He who belongs to God hears what God says. The reason you do not hear is that you do not belong to God."</u> (John 8:47)

Remember, too, the advice we received in the book of Psalms concerning sin:

If I had cherished sin in my heart, the Lord would not have listened. But God has surely listened and heard my voice in prayer. *Praise be to God, who has not rejected my prayer or withheld His love from me!* (Psalm 66:18-20)

And finally, in first Peter chapter 3, verse 12:

For the eyes of the Lord are on the righteous and his ears are attentive to their prayer, but the face of the Lord is against those who do evil.

6. Breaking Down Roadblocks

On the contrary, the Word tells us in Proverbs 15:8 tells us that *the prayer of the upright pleases Him.*

It's important to remember that this term: righteous – is not about us being perfect, but instead about us having a heart that truly "seeks first the kingdom of God". Sometimes we don't connect a seemingly small or insignificant sin with a lack of answer to prayer. Sometimes we don't even realize that we are indeed sinning! Most Christians love the Lord and work diligently at being obedient, not even realizing that they may be walking in sin in certain areas. So I'm going to cover here a few of the more common sins that are roadblocks to our prayer.

1. **Unforgiveness.** This is a tough area to conquer in this earthly world. So many of us have been hurt terribly by others - serious, damaging hurts that have caused unimaginable pain. One of the most compelling verses in the Word that helped me with unforgiveness that I had harbored was found in Matthew, chapter 6:

    "For if you forgive men when they sin against you, your heavenly Father will also forgive you. But if you do not forgive men their sins, your Father will not forgive your sins." (Matthew 6:14-15)

    This was one of those verses that was a "wake-up call" for me. My right and my reason for being angry and unforgiving toward the people who had hurt me seemed pretty insignificant when I realized that my unforgiveness could make the difference between my eternity in Heaven and my eternity in Hell. In the book of Mark, God shows how our unforgiveness can hinder our prayers:

<u>*And when you stand praying, if you hold anything against anyone, forgive him, so that your Father in Heaven may forgive your sins.*</u>" (Mark 11:25)

Many of us have been hurt by terrible, unchangeable sins that others have done to us; hurts grander than most people could even imagine. The great deception of unforgiveness, however, is that it only hurts the holder of it. It has even been shown to make humans physically sick! Make a choice, daily, hourly, or whenever the Enemy tries to put unforgiveness in your heart, to choose to forgive, and let vengeance be God's. Say out loud for the Enemy to hear: *Devil, I reject your spirit of unforgiveness. I have forgiven _____.* Say it every time you feel unforgiveness trying to sneak into your heart. Not only will this heal your soul and your body; it will allow God to once again fill your heart with joy. Then take it one step further, and pray for God's blessings upon the ones that have hurt you. This step will this further crush the Enemy's plans to stifle your life with his spirit of unforgiveness, it will also bring a blessing on you, as the word says in First Peter chapter 3:8-9

Finally, all of you, be of one mind, having compassion for one another; love as brothers, be tenderhearted,

6. Breaking Down Roadblocks

be courteous; not returning evil for evil, or reviling for reviling, but on the contrary blessing, knowing that you were called to this, that you may inherit a blessing.

Make a commitment to walk in forgiveness, then watch and see your life prosper - body, soul and spirit!

2. **Pride.** Pride is another area that hinders our prayers. You can tell that pride is of the Enemy's camp because it makes us believe we are better than others. Anytime our mind is telling us that our sins, our life, our possessions, our family, or whatever, is better than other people's, the focus is on us, and therefore off of God. This was Satan's sin from the beginning. He thought he could do a better job of running the universe than God and purposed in his heart to take over. Just as his sin of pride thousands of years ago caused his separation from the Lord, our sins of pride today will do the same thing. Pride causes us to think that we don't need God, and that we can do a fine job of running our lives ourselves. But remember that God sees all and knows all. Who better to have as your guide and your protector? Let's look and see what the Word has to say about pride:

To fear the Lord is to hate evil. I hate pride and arrogance, evil behavior and perverse speech. (Proverbs 8:13)

Proverbs 16:18 tells us that *"Pride goes before destruction, and a haughty spirit before a fall."*

Now let's look at the blessings that come with humility, which is the opposite of pride:

The wise men of the Old Testament tell us:

The Lord's curse is on the house of the wicked, but He blesses the home of the righteous. He mocks proud mockers, but gives grace to the humble. (Proverbs 3:33-34)

Good and upright is the Lord; therefore He instructs sinners in His ways. He guides the humble in what is right and teaches them His way. (Psalm 25:8-9)

<u>"This is the one I esteem;"</u> says the Lord," <u>he who is humble and contrite in spirit, and trembles at my word."</u> (Isaiah 66:2)

Paul urges us in Ephesians:

As a prisoner for the Lord, then, I urge you to live a life worthy of the calling you have received. Be completely humble and gentle; be patient, bearing with one another in love. (Ephesians 4:1-2)

James encourages us to:

Humble yourselves before the Lord, and He will lift you up. (James 4:10)

Paul shows us in Philippians how Jesus' humility caused Him to be crowned the Name above all names:

6. Breaking Down Roadblocks

And being found in appearance as a man, He (Jesus) humbled Himself and became obedient to death - even death on a cross! Therefore God exalted Him to the highest place and gave Him the name that is above every name. (Philippians 2:8-9)

And Jesus Himself showed us that:

<u>*For whoever exalts himself will be humbled, and whoever humbles himself will be exalted*</u>. (Matthew 23:12)

The great thing about humility is that it allows you to see:

1. Your need for God
2. God's greatness
3. Your weaknesses

and possibly most importantly, it helps you to be more diligent in earnestly seeking His ways, because it's easier to see that you need Him. Humility, you see, helps us to see that we are better off letting the God who knows all lead our lives. This "stepping back" and letting God take the controls allows Him to show us His ways, and subsequently allows God to guide us into His best for us, provided we're willing to ask for and listen to His instruction. So, humility, which seems at the outset to be a form of weakness, is truly a grand form of power that will indeed guide your life into places you could only have dreamed of! Choose today to walk in humility and let God be God of your life. The wisdom and blessings that will follow this choice will be poured out on you more graciously than you ever could have imagined!

3. **A Lack of Faith.** Although this may seem like more of a spiritual defect than a sin, the Word makes it clear that faith is in our control, and that a lack of it displeases God immensely. Let's review one of the verses we covered in Chapter 5 about a lack of faith and how it displeases God:

A man in the crowd answered, "Teacher, I brought you my son, who is possessed by a spirit that has robbed him of speech. Whenever it seizes him, it throws him to the ground. He foams at the mouth, gnashes his teeth and becomes rigid. I asked your disciples to drive out the spirit, but they could not. "<u>O, unbelieving generation</u>," Jesus replied, "<u>how long shall I stay with you? How long must I put up with you? Bring the boy to me.</u>" (Mark 9:17-19).

When you read that story, can't you just feel the contempt and irritation in the Lord's voice? These are *His* disciples, who have been with Him day and night for quite some time now. They've even been sent out themselves and performed miracles and healed the sick (Mark 6)! He expects, after all of the miracles they've seen – and all of the miracles they've done themselves - that they would *"get it"*, and His tone makes it clear that He is displeased that they don't.

6. Breaking Down Roadblocks

Remember that it says in Hebrews that: *without faith it is impossible to please God, because anyone who comes to Him must believe that He exists and that He rewards those who earnestly seek Him.* (Hebrews 11:6)

So it is clear, then, that in order to please the Lord we must have faith, and since faith is considered an act of obedience, then a lack of faith must be viewed as sin, as written in the book of Romans:

But the man who has doubts is condemned if he eats, because his eating is not from faith, and ***everything that does not come from faith is sin.*** (Romans 14:23)

Faith, it's true, must be learned, nurtured, and grown, but God has given us a **choice as to whether to do that or not.** Now, there are some arguments in the church about whether or not God gives His children the same measures of faith, or gives us all different measures of faith. These arguments are based largely on Romans 12:3, which reads in part:

Do not think of yourself more highly that you ought, but rather think of yourself with sober judgment, in accordance with the measure of faith God has given you. (Romans 12:3)

Now, some see this verse to mean that God has given each of us a different measure of faith, and others take it to mean that God has given us each the same measure of faith. Regardless of one's interpretation of the verse, however, there are many, many verses in the Bible that make it clear that faith is like a muscle, needing to be strengthened and grown, that we have the power within us to grow our faith, and that - most importantly - God *expects* us to grow our faith! Since *faith comes by hearing, and hearing by the Word of God* (Romans 10:17), make a choice to get into the Word today - and every day - and increase your faith!

4. **Disobedience to God's instruction.** It's funny sometimes, the process of learning to listen to God. God works with us at our human level in this area - one step at a time. When you ask the Lord to help you discern His voice, the first instructions you hear may not be quite what you expected. He may say simple, seemingly irrelevant things, like *hold the door open for this person,* or *go this different route home today.* While these seemingly insignificant instructions may not make sense to you, you'll soon come to realize that in many of the cases the Lord is simply *training* you to hear and obey His voice and instruction. The Word tells us that:

Whoever can be trusted with very little can also be trusted with very much. (Luke 16:10)

The Lord works with us slowly. He gives us these seemingly small commands, and He will keep giving us these small commands, until we learn to listen and obey them. Then, as we learn to hear and obey His voice, those commands will get bigger and more significant. Because God loves us, however, He will only give us commands according to what we can handle. Just as you don't give a 5-year old a driver's license, God won't give a Christian who's just starting to hear His voice and obey His Word a giant, earth-moving command. God knows what you can handle, and in His love and graciousness, He'll never give you a job that's too big for you or that you're not ready for.

Once you've become more proficient at hearing and obeying His voice and His commands, however, He will expect more of you, and there are natural consequences for disobedience in this area. Remember what we learned about disobedience and its effects on prayer earlier in the chapter:

<u>"If My people, who are called my My Name, will humble themselves and pray and seek My face, and turn from their wicked ways, then will I hear from Heaven and will forgive their sin and will heal their land.</u> **<u>Now my eyes will be open and my ears attentive to the prayers offered in this place.</u>** (2 Chronicles 7:14-15)

If I had cherished sin in my heart, the Lord would not have listened. But God has surely listened and heard my voice in prayer. *Praise be to God, who has not rejected my prayer or withheld His love from me!* (Psalm 66:18-20)

If you are having trouble hearing from the Lord, or if you feel in your spirit there is a blockage to your communication with Him, recall the last few instructions that He gave you, and check to see if you carried them out fully. Or ask for His wisdom if you're having trouble remembering whether or not you've not fulfilled an instruction He gave you. If you haven't, go back and correct the situation and do what the Lord told you to do. Just as a plumber who clears a clogged pipe allows the water to once again run freely, this self-check and correction of any disobeyed commands will open up the lines of communication with the Lord, and He will once again hear your prayers.

5. **Not walking in love**. This is an area where many, many Christians "miss the boat". Strife and hatred will always separate you from God and close His ears to your prayers. Let's see what the Word says about this. The book of Proverbs says about strife that:

It is to a man's honor to avoid strife, but every fool is quick to quarrel. (Proverbs 20:3)

Drive out the mocker and out goes strife; quarrels and insults are ended. (Proverbs 22:10)

But about love, it says:

Let love and faithfulness never leave you; bind them around your neck, write them on the tablet of your heart. **Then you will win favor and a good name in the sight of God and man.** (Proverbs 3: 3-4)

Hatred stirs up strife, but love covers all sins. (Proverbs 10:12)

Love and faithfulness keep a king safe; through love his throne is made secure. (Proverbs 20:28)

He who pursues righteousness and love finds life, prosperity and honor. (Proverbs 21:21)

The book of Isaiah says about Jesus' coming that:

In love a throne will be established; in faithfulness a man will sit on it - one from the house of David - one who in judging seeks justice and speeds the cause of righteousness. (Isaiah 16:5)

If you are having trouble getting your prayers answered, check your "love life". Is there someone you are harboring feelings of hate or anger toward? If so, regardless of the issue that has caused this anger, there are things that you can do to heal your heart and replace that anger or hurt with love.

First, ask the Lord's forgiveness for the wrong feelings you've been holding onto. Secondly, ask the Lord to help you see that person as He sees them. This will give you a new outlook, not only on that person, but also on the situation that caused your feelings of anger toward them in the first place.

Third, and probably most importantly, purpose in your heart today to start doing things for that person that will confirm the love that you have in your heart for them. This is the **faith action step** that will help your love for them truly become a reality. Send them a nice card, help them with something they need help with, or simply pray for God's blessings and protection over them. As you do more and more things in love for that person, or persons, you will find that your love for them truly does grow, and regardless of whether or not that person returns the love that you are showing them, *you* will be in right standing with God. Then you will once again make sure that your lines of communication to Him are open, putting you back in that position of getting answered prayers.

6. **Idolatry**. This is a roadblock that often goes unnoticed and under the radar of our spiritual instinct. The main reason for this, I believe, is because we don't have a clear understanding of what idolatry is. We think of idolatry as worshiping other gods, or having a religion other than Christianity, but the term "other gods" consists of more than just those gods that you hear about from other religions. People can fall into idolatry with money, sports, their spouses, their kids, their houses, cars, jobs, or anything else on this earth. The Word is very clear:

Anyone who loves his father or mother more than me is not worthy of me; anyone who loves his son or daughter more than me is not worthy of me; and anyone who does not take his cross and follow me is not worthy of me. Whoever finds his life will lose it, and whoever loses his life for my sake will find it. (Matthew 10:37-38)

And again in Matthew 6 Jesus tells us that:

No one can serve two masters. Either he will hate the one and love the other, or he will be devoted to the one and despise the other. You cannot serve both God and money. (Matthew 6:24)

When Jesus is talking here about losing your life, He isn't speaking literally. He's asking the question: *Who is it that you truly serve? If it is I, you will find true life, if it is not, you will find despair and hell.*

In this day and age, too, it's easy to worship other things even if you don't want to. If you are in bondage from debt and working day and night to get out, money, your job and debt are your masters. If you do so much for your spouse and your kids that you don't have time for the Lord, your family is your master. If caring for your house or your cars comes before God and before your family, the house and the cars are your master. The Enemy can even use work in the church to lead us into idolatry. Many a man and woman spend so much time in their church work or other ministry work that God and their families are a distant second and third. Serving at the church or in any other ministry cannot replace your time alone with God. God must come first, and there is a simple remedy to these traps that are so easy to fall into: *Choose to seek first the kingdom of God and His righteousness* - every day (Matthew 6:33). This is why devoting the first minutes/hours of your day to the Lord is so very important. First, it shows God that He truly has first place in your life. Second, it gets your focus where it needs to be: on the Lord. Third, when you start your day getting focused on Him and spending time with Him, you will receive the wisdom and the clarity that will teach you how to manage every other area of your life in success and peace! It is an assurance that you are in right relationship with God, and will allow for your prayers to be heard, as well as answered.

7. **Not treating your body as the Temple of the Holy Spirit**. Do you treat yourself and your body the same way that you would've treated Jesus' body had He been born to you? Put yourself, for a minute, in Mary's place. It's 2011, and you have been entrusted with raising the Son of God. What would you feed him? Would you allow His precious body to be filled with the chemicals that we see in much of today's food? Would you allow his mind to be littered with violent movies and video games? Would you allow Him to spend His days on the couch, void of any physical exercise? I can't imagine you would. I would hope that anyone that the Lord would entrust with raising His Son in these days would take precious care of that boy, making

sure that His mind, body and spirit are filled with the Lord's goodness and His goodness only. So why do we treat our own bodies any differently? Let's take another look at the Word and see what God says about our bodies and minds:

Do you not know that your bodies are members of Christ Himself? Do you not know that your body is a temple of the Holy Spirit, who is in you, whom you have received from God? You are not your own, you were bought at a price. Therefore honor God with your body. (1 Corinthians 6:15, 19, 20)

I beseech you therefore, brethren, by the mercies of God, that you present your bodies a living sacrifice, holy, acceptable to God, which is your reasonable service. And do not be conformed to this world, but be transformed by the renewing of your mind (with the Word of God), *that you may prove what is the good and acceptable and perfect will of God.* (Romans 12:1-2)

Do not offer the parts of your body to sin, as instruments of wickedness, but rather offer yourselves to God.... (Romans 6:13)

For we are the temple of the living God. As God has said: <u>I will live with them and walk among them, and I will be their God, and they will be my people. Therefore come out from them and be separate. Touch no unclean thing, and I will receive you. I will be a Father to you, and you will be my sons and daughters,</u>" says *the Lord Almighty. Therefore, having these promises, beloved, let us cleanse ourselves from all filthiness of the flesh and spirit, perfecting holiness in the fear of God.* (2 Corinthians 6:16-18, 7:1)

Treating yourself as the temple of God consists of guarding your physical body as well as your spirit and your soul. If we are to truly treat our bodies as God's temple, then we must guard what comes into our minds as well as what comes into our mouths. A good way to guard what comes into your mind is to put everything you choose to read or watch or see up against the verse in Philippians 4:8:

Finally, brethren, whatever is true, noble, just, pure, lovely, of good report, or anything praiseworthy - think on these things.

Use this measure to discern every book you read, every show you watch, and every conversation you choose to enter. If what you are hearing, reading or seeing does not fall under the guidelines stated in Philippians 4:8, I would urge you to strongly reconsider whether or not you want that information in the temple of the Holy Spirit. **You see, whatever we put *into* our hearts will come out of our hearts.** Therefore, we must guard carefully against putting things that are contrary to God's Word in our hearts. This will help ensure that when we pray, we are praying God's Word and God's will, and not the will or the lies of the Enemy.

6. Breaking Down Roadblocks

What we put in our physical bodies can have the same negative impact on our prayers. If you are filling your body with processed, chemical-filled foods, instead of the foods God gave us, your body and your mind will not function with the same wisdom and clarity that God means it to. Try this test: For 7 days, eat only whole foods: raw or steamed fruits and veggies, nuts, lean meats, brown organic rice, and small amounts of dairy like milk, cheese and butter. Avoid sugar, white flour, and processed foods of any kind. Watch and monitor your mind and body and see how you feel at the end of those 7 days. For the first 3 days or so, you may see symptoms of withdrawal, such as crabbiness, fatigue, or headaches, as your body clears itself from the addictive additives we put in our processed foods. By the end of day 7, however, you should notice a much clearer, calmer mind and body. You'll see things differently. Fear and anger will melt away. Love will overtake your heart. Imagine the impact this will have on your prayers! It will give you a more unified relationship with the Lord, as your body will be more clean and aligned spiritually with His, and it will allow for your mind to more clearly hear His will, so you can pray with more clarity, strength, and assurance that you and He are on the same page.

Although that on the outset, what you eat and put into your mind may seem irrelevant in regard to your prayer life, you'll soon find that changing how you treat your body will boost your prayer life in a way that you've never imagined. Try it today and see!

8. **Not taming your tongue**. This may be one of the most crucial roadblocks that we encounter in prayer today. Let's talk a bit first about what the Word says about the words we speak:

Let the words of my mouth and the meditation of my heart be acceptable in your sight, O Lord, my strength and my Redeemer. (Psalm 19:14)

I said, "I will guard my ways lest I sin with my tongue; I will put a muzzle on my mouth as long as the wicked are in my presence." (Psalm 39:1)

There is one who speaks like the piercings of a sword, but the tongue of the wise brings healing. Truthful lips endure forever, but a lying tongue lasts only a moment. (Proverbs 12:18-19)

If anyone considers himself religious and yet does not keep a tight rein on his tongue, he deceives himself and his religion is worthless. (James 1:26)

He who guards his lips guards his life, but he who speaks rashly will come to ruin. (Proverbs 13:3)

But now you must rid yourselves of all such things as these: anger, rage, malice, slander and filthy language from your lips. (Colossians 3:8)

6. Breaking Down Roadblocks

A wise man's heart guides his mouth, and his lips promote instruction. (Proverbs 16:23)

All kinds of animals, birds, reptiles and creatures of the sea are being tamed and have been tamed by man, but no man can tame the tongue. It is a restless evil, full of deadly poison. With the tongue we praise our Lord and Father, and with it we curse men, who have been made in God's likeness. Out of the same mouth come praise and cursing. My brothers, this should not be! Can both fresh water and salt water flow from the same spring? My brothers, can a fig tree bear olives, or a grapevine bear figs? Neither can a salt spring produce fresh water. (James 3:7-12)

You brood of vipers, how can you who are evil say anything good? For out of the overflow of the heart the mouth speaks. (Matthew 12:34)

The Bible is clear here that our words have power. Remember what we learned in Mark chapter 11: "<u>Have faith in God. I tell you the truth, if anyone says to this mountain, 'Go, throw yourself into the sea,' and does not doubt in his heart but believes that what he says will happen, he will have whatever he says.</u>" (Mark 11:23)

If you are praying for one thing, and then going out into the world and saying another, you will indeed *have what you say*. Let's say, for example, that you are standing and praying for healing from a terrible cold. If you spend your day grumbling and complaining and walking in pity, saying "I'm SO sick, I'm so, so sick! I always get a cold this time of the year." you will not see the immediate healing that Jesus saw when He laid His hands on the people. Why? Because you are saying, proclaiming, that you are indeed sick and that you always get sick! Does that seem silly or unrealistic to you? The Word says that you will *have whatever you say!* Go back and read the healing stories of Jesus in the Bible. He never said, "You are sick". He said, "You are healed." He said, "According to your faith it will be done to you." He said, "Your faith has healed you." He spoke the truth - *He spoke the Word of God, and the Word of God says that "by His stripes, you are healed"*!

I got a first-hand dose of reality about "having what I say" just recently in our house. One of my fervent prayers to the Lord the last several months has been that He would show me how to have the faith and the wisdom to heal like Jesus healed, as the Bible said we would do. The growth and understanding in this area has been slow for me, but we are finally starting to get glimpses and examples of healing with our words. One example happened about 6 weeks ago when my 8-year old daughter had an earring rip out of her ear in her sleep. This was not a dangly earring, but a stud earring that contained a stone. One of the prongs apparently got caught on something as she slept, and the earring ripped her ear lobe right in half. We just left the lobe, hoping it would grow back together on its own. When it didn't, we consulted some physicians, and some friends who had had similar injuries, and learned that surgery would be required to repair the ear. As my daughter requested, I scheduled the surgery, and then went to the Lord seeking healing before our surgery consult date so that surgery wouldn't be necessary. Imagine my excitement a week later when I looked at my daughter's ear, and saw that the cut was about half-way sealed up! In my shock, I said, "I can't believe it!" I looked at the ear again, and said again, "I can't believe it! I can't believe it!" Then I watched as the healed top half of the ear came apart, right before my eyes! The Lord immediately convicted me of my error and reminded me that I "can have whatever I say". I felt horrible! Here, with my words, I had undone the glorious work God had done for my daughter.

When you are talking - in prayer, and out of prayer - say what God says. Don't say what the Enemy says. The Enemy says you are sick, sad, and that you live a miserable life. Jesus says *"I have come that they may have life, and have it abundantly"*! Make sure your words, in prayer and out of prayer, always line up with what the Word of God says about who you are in Jesus Christ. Remember: the only weapon the Enemy has is the power to deceive us into believing that we have no power in Jesus Christ. But Luke 10:19 says *that God has given us authority over ALL the power of the Enemy and nothing, by any means, shall harm us!* Praise the Lord - He is the Great Deliverer! Get to know the Word today, and then speak what Jesus speaks. If you are praying and standing for a situation to change, say what you want, not what you have. This is not deceiving yourself or lying if you are speaking what the Word says; no, this is standing on God's truth over the world's truth. Too many people don't let the Bible get in the way of what they believe, opting instead to believe the world over the Word. However, Hebrews 11 tells us that *faith is the substance of things hoped for, the evidence of things not seen.* The book of James Chapter 4 *tells us to "submit yourselves to God and resist the Devil, and he will flee from you".* Tame your tongue and train your mind so that your words always match up with what the Bible says is God's will for your life. Your prayers will have more power than they've ever had before!

9. **Envy.** Envy, or covetousness, is one of the great hidden sins that can hinder our prayer life, and the rest of our life, many times without us even realizing what's going on. The main problem with envy is that it gets your focus off of God, onto yourself and onto the world. Again, this will put confusion into your mind, making it difficult to have clear communication with the Lord. The Enemy does a very good job of putting messages into our minds that tell us that our lives are terrible and that everyone around us has it better than us - a better marriage, better kids, better job, better stuff, and when you allow yourself to believe those lies, you start to speak them and you start to focus on them. Having had years of experience praying for others, I can assure you that the lives of those whom you see as so much

6. Breaking Down Roadblocks

better than yours are filled with many struggles as well. In my years in mortgage and personal banking, I would often come across people who made hundreds of thousands of dollars a year - people who looked, from a materialistic standpoint, like they "had it all". They were, however, struggling and in debt just as much as my clients who made only the so-called "poverty level" income. I've seen the same revelations with people who looked like they had it all in their marriage, their children, their jobs and everything else. We all struggle in some area or another, and those who truly are not struggling the way the rest of us are are likely in that position due to spending a great amount of time with the Lord and in His Word, thereby gaining the knowledge and wisdom from Him on how to live His way. They've learned how to let God give them the wisdom to *make all their "paths peace."* (Proverbs 3:17)

The best cure that I have found for covetousness is ministry. You think you've got it bad? Go spend an afternoon serving food to the homeless, or packing food to send to third world countries. Go and complete a Habitat for Humanity or other project. Watch a documentary on the lack of clean water in Africa, and the perils that people need to overcome just to have water to drink. You'll soon see that there are many, many people in the world that have it so much worse than you do.

We do a simple activity in our family, often while driving in the car, that is a great cure for envy and self-pity and brings praise to the Lord at the same time, and here's how it works: We take turns, starting with one person and going in a circle, thanking Him. We start our sentences saying "I thank you, Lord, for…" We "do our rounds" like this at least 5 or 6 times, until we've all got happy hearts and a good remembrance of all of the blessings we've been given. Sometimes our thanks is for things we already have, like food, water, shelter, family, and sometimes our thanks is for things we are standing together for, like healing for someone or for deliverance for someone or something. One thing I can tell you for sure, though, is that this simple activity gets us off of the "envy and self-focus" track and back onto the "giving all of the glory to God" track quickly.

Having a clean heart before God really does make a grand difference in answered prayers and unanswered prayers. Decide today to rid your lives of the sins that may be hindering your prayers, and see for yourself how it will free you in ways that you've never even dreamed of!

Enemy attacks.

This is the other major roadblock to answered prayers. Let's look in the book of Daniel to find how God's Word explains this:

In the third year of Cyrus king of Persia, a revelation was given to Daniel. Its message was true and in concerned a great war. The understanding of the message came to him in a vision. At that time, I, Daniel, mourned for three weeks. I ate no choice food; no meat or wine touched my lips; and I used no lotions at all until the three weeks were over. (Daniel 10: 1-3) Daniel did this as he prayed to the Lord for wisdom, understanding and help regarding the vision he was given. We pick up again in verse 10:

A hand touched me and set me trembling on my hands and knees. He said, "Daniel, you who are highly esteemed, consider carefully the words I am about to speak to you, and stand up, for I (I refers to the "certain man" who was sent to Daniel - some believe this is a high-ranking angel, and some, noting his description in prior verses is remarkably like John's description of Jesus in the book of Revelation. Those believing it was a high-ranking angel, however, have a good point in maintaining that Jesus would not have needed to battle against Satan because of His great power) *have now been sent to you. And when he said this to me, I stood up trembling. Then he continued, "Do not be afraid, Daniel. Since the first day that you set your mind* (in prayer) *to gain understanding and to humble yourself before your God, your words were heard, and I have come in response to them. But the prince of the Persian kingdom* (Satan) *resisted me twenty-one days. Then Michael, one of the chief princes, came to help me, because I was detained there with the king of Persia.*

Some people in the world today have no problem believing in God, but they think the idea of the Devil is nothing more than a ridiculous story. This may well be the Enemy's greatest deception - convincing people that he doesn't exist. There are great dangers in believing that God is responsible for and has ordained all of the evil acts in this world. First, if you don't know and understand and put the blame where it belongs, you give the Enemy continued free reign to wreak havoc on your life. Second, you make God out to be a horrible master, and send people running from Him as fast as they can.

Let's look and see what the Bible says about Satan:

Be self-controlled and alert. **Your enemy the devil prowls around like a roaring lion looking for someone to devour.** *Resist him, standing firm in the faith....* (1 Peter 5:8-9)

The thief comes only to steal, kill and destroy; *I have come that they may have life, and have it abundantly.* (John 10:10)

The great dragon was hurled down-that ancient serpent called the devil, or **Satan, who leads the whole world astray**. (Rev. 12:9)

Satan, it's clear, is the bad guy. God is the good guy! Remember Jeremiah 29:11. It says:

<u>"For I know the plans I have for you,"</u> says the Lord. <u>Plans of good and not evil, to give you a future and a hope."</u>

So many people mistakenly give God the blame for the evil done on this earth when the blame lies squarely with the Devil! The Lord gave me a very clear picture of this some years ago as I attended the funeral of a bright, beautiful little boy who had been killed in an accident.

As I stood there, looking at the casket and praying for this little one and his family, the Lord said to me: *This is how evil the Devil is. You know that I love my people with a love that could never be surpassed - a love that humans could never imagine. Well, the Devil hates humans with a hate that could never be surpassed - a hate that no one can imagine. Any being that would steal the life of an innocent little boy and take pleasure in it is filled to the brim, overflowing with hate.* **You must never underestimate the Enemy's hate for people.** *This is why it is crucial if you are to rise above his attacks that you be vigilant at all times. You must know thoroughly who he is, and that he is here only to steal, kill and destroy, and you must be on your guard at all times. Never let your guard down, not even for a moment. Stand on the blood of Jesus, plead it over your families and all that you own and do. Know my Word and use the instructions in it given to defeat him.*

The Devil certainly does have only death and destruction in mind, but praise the Lord, He sent His son, because:

For this purpose the Son of God was manifested, that He might destroy the works of the devil. (1 John 3:8)

<u>*Behold, I have given you authority over all the power of the Enemy, and nothing – by any means – shall harm you.*</u> (Luke 10:19)

<u>*"My prayer is not that you take them out of the world, but that you protect them from the evil one."*</u> (John 17:15)

It's only when we are unaware of our enemies – and unaware that we have power over them - that they can gain a foothold, but the Lord gives us the help and instruction we need to stay above the Devil's schemes. Let's look and see what He says to do:

Submit yourselves, then, to God. Resist the devil and he will flee from you. (James 4:7)

I am sending you out like sheep among wolves. Therefore be as cunning as serpents, and as gentle as doves. (Matthew 10:16)

Finally, be strong in the Lord and in His mighty power. Put on the full armor of God so that you can take your stand against the wiles of the devil. (Ephesians 6:10-11).

Now, Jesus was the only sinless person ever to exist on the face of this earth. Because of that, He remained completely out of the Enemy's reach until His ordained time to die on the cross, and not because the Enemy didn't try to trap Him. So let's look at Jesus' example of how to live a life free of the Enemy. What did Jesus do to accomplish this?

-He kept His life sin-free and walked in total obedience to God. If you'll do a thorough reading of the four gospels, it's quite clear that Jesus sought first the kingdom of God and His righteousness. Even when He didn't want to, He did it anyway. He asked the Lord if He might change His path, but when push came to shove, His attitude was "not my will, but yours, be done." Let's look at Jesus' time in the Garden of Gethsemane:

6. Breaking Down Roadblocks

Then Jesus went with His disciples to a place called Gethsemane, and he said to them, "<u>Sit here while I go over there and pray.</u>" He took Peter and the two sons of Zebedee along with Him, and He began to be sorrowful and troubled. Then He said to them, "<u>My soul is overwhelmed with sorrow to the point of death. Stay here and keep watch with me</u>." Going a little farther, He fell with His face to the ground and prayed, "<u>My Father, if it is possible, may this cup be taken from me. Yet, not as I will, but your will be done.</u>"(Matthew 26:36-39)

Jesus' fear and sorrow here about his death on the cross is so very evident. He even went to the Lord a second time to ask that this "cup be taken away" from Him. In the end, however, He always submitted to the Lord, saying "not my will be done, but yours."

We talked in Chapter 5 about the many verses in the Word that admonish and encourage us to live a sin-free life. Although we will never be completely sin-free until the arrival of the new heaven and the new earth, it is completely in our power to do our very best to try to follow the leadings of our spirit as opposed to the lusts of our flesh, and to grow in righteousness each and every day. You may be saved by grace and going to heaven because of it - regardless of your sin - but keeping out of the Enemy's camp by living in obedience to God's Word will allow for a much better life here on earth. Choosing to accept your various sins as simply a part of being in a fallen world is nothing more than a deception of the Enemy. Why else would the Word speak so strongly to us about rejecting sin? Remember what we learned about sin in Romans chapter 6:

*What shall we say, then**? Shall we go on sinning so that grace many increase? By no means! We died to sin; how can we live in it any longer?** Or don't you know that all of us who were baptized into Christ Jesus were baptized into His death? We were therefore buried with Him through baptism into death in order that, just as Christ was raised from the dead, through the glory of the Father, we too may live a new life.*

*If we have been united with Him like this in His death, we will certainly also be united with Him in His resurrection. For we know that our old self was crucified with him so that the body of sin might be done away with, that we **should no longer be slaves to sin** - because anyone who has died has been freed from sin…*

Disciplining yourself to work towards a sin-free and obedient life does take work. It will require you to give up some long-held habits, to take a good, long look at your heart and **to train yourself to follow your spirit instead of your flesh,** but the trade-offs are immeasurable. Remember what we were taught in the book of James:

The prayer of a righteous man is powerful and effective and avails much. (James 5:16)

Walking on God's path instead of the Devil's will bring you a peace, safety and joy that you never dreamed existed here on earth. Ask the Lord to guide you in this process. Ask Him to show you where there is sin in your life and how to correct it. Learn through the Word how you can follow your spirit instead of your flesh. We often think of our sins as "little" compared to the sins of unsaved world, but sin is sin. They're all the same in God's eyes, and they all put us on the Devil's path for us instead of on God's path for us. So make a commitment today to go to the Word and to find out what God's will is for your behavior. Then follow it.

-He spent lots and lots of time with the Lord. The Bible talks many times about how Jesus *went away to be with the Lord,* or *withdrew to a quiet place to pray.*

> A thorough examination of the four gospels will show you that prayer and fellowship was the cornerstone of Jesus' relationship with God, and that it was Jesus' strength to get through all things successfully.
>
> Jesus was committed - totally and completely - to doing what the Lord wanted Him to do, even to the point of death on a cross! When Jesus came to this earth, born as a babe, the Word tells us that he needed to – and did – grow in wisdom and in stature (Luke 2:52). He knew, too, that the more time He spent in prayer, praise and fellowship with God, the more He would fully understand God's will and plan for His life. We should strive for that same commitment to God. Although it may seem on the outset that committing to spend more time with the Lord will be a sacrifice, you'll find after just a

short time living in obedience to God's instruction by seeking Him first that you'll have a peace and a protection that will far surpass any "sacrifice" your extra time with the Lord takes.

-He walked in love. This is likely the most crucial aspect of obedience that we can strive for in getting our prayers heard and answered, and for walking in God's protection. Some may argue that Jesus spent time rebuking and disciplining the people as well as showing love to them, and they'd be totally correct. The underlying theme in Jesus' rebuke and correction, though, was always love! Let's look at Jesus' rebuke of the Pharisees in the book of Matthew:

> *You snakes! You brood of vipers! How will you escape being condemned to hell? Therefore I am sending you prophets and wise men and teachers. Some of them you will kill and crucify; others you will flog in your synagogues and pursue from town to town. And so upon you will come all the righteous blood that has been shed on earth, from the blood of righteous Abel to the blood of Zechariah son of Berekiah, whom you murdered between the temple and the altar. I tell you the truth, all of this will come upon this generation.* (Matthew 23:33-36)

But look at His follow up statement:

> *O Jerusalem, Jerusalem, you who kill the prophets and stone those sent to you, how often I have*

6. Breaking Down Roadblocks

longed to gather your children together, as a hen gathers her chicks under her wings, but you were not willing." (Matthew 23:37)

Can't you just feel His great love for the people as He pleads with them? **But they chose to continue in sin and disobedience.** This broke His heart, but it was their choice, not His. As much as this pained Jesus, He knew that He had to just do His job - love them and urge them to repent - and let them make their choices. His love for them, however, never ceased. Walking in love keeps you on God's path and off of the Enemy's path for your life, because we as humans need God close by in order to truly walk in love.

-He let the Lord lead. Another important step that Jesus took in His life here on earth was that He worked hard to know (through time spent in prayer with the Lord) exactly what the Lord wanted Him to do in each and every step of His life, and He did it. Jesus didn't make His decisions - even the smallest of ones - based on what He wanted. He made them based on what *God* wanted. When we follow His example, we again stay on God's path and off of the path of the Enemy.

Learn to ask the Lord for discernment and wisdom and His will with everything you do. This may seem silly, and even a bit over the top at first. But the Lord has a perfect plan for you, and even one decision outside of His will can take you far off of His path. Those of you who have already had some experience in learning to discern His voice can most certainly think of at least one time when something less than desirable happened in your life, and, looking back, realized that you did indeed have that check in your spirit from the Lord that told you to stop and reconsider. I can say this about nearly every troubled event in my life since I've learned to hear and obey His voice. Every time I try to do things my way, without God as my consultant, I end up heading on a course that I don't want to be on. When I ask Him for His wishes, however, even for the smallest of decisions, my life is much more wrinkle-free.

This is not to say that you should live in fear of making mistakes or going off of His path, because, praise the Lord, we have His grace in our times of error, and He will always guide you back onto His path if you ask Him to. Learning, however, to seek God's will in everything we do will give us a clearer understanding of His ways, and a clearer understanding of the Enemy's ways, therefore allowing us to make choices that please God and keep us and our families safe in the refuge of the shadow of His wings.

6. Breaking Down Roadblocks

God is a *good God.* He wants nothing more than for you to walk in the love and the blessings He has for you. Learn to recognize and break down the roadblocks to getting your prayers heard and answered, and you'll soon taste and see that the Lord is indeed good! (Psalm 34:8)

7. Protection with Prayer

With the increase in unrest and violence in today's world, God's protection is of great concern and importance to many people. In order to pray properly for protection, however, it is crucial that you know and understand God's will for your life and the lives of those that you are praying for when it comes to protection.

The Word is very clear that God's plan for our lives is a good plan - a safe one! This does not mean that we will not endure trials, but it does mean that if we follow God's will, we can increase our chances of coming out of those trials safely.

So what is God's will? In order to find that out, we must look at the Word, and learn the root of good, and the root of evil. If you don't pull a weed out by the root, it just grows back, correct? Let's start in Deuteronomy 28 to see what God promises to those who follow Him:

If you fully obey the Lord your God and carefully follow all His commands I give you today, the Lord your God will set you high above all the nations on earth. All of these blessings will come upon you and accompany you if you obey the Lord your God:

You will be blessed in the city and blessed in the country.

The fruit of your womb will be blessed, and the crops of your land and the young of your livestock - the calves of your herds and the lambs of your flocks.

Your basket and your kneading trough will be blessed.

You will be blessed when you come in and blessed when you go out.

The Lord will grant that the enemies who rise up against you will be defeated before you. They will come at you from one direction but flee from you in seven. The Lord will send a blessing on your barns and on everything you put your hand to. The Lord your God will bless you in the land He is giving you. The Lord will establish you as His holy people, as He promised you on oath, if you keep the commands of the Lord your God and walk in His ways.

7. Protection with Prayer

Then all the peoples on earth will see that you are called by the name of the Lord and they will fear you. The Lord will grant you abundant prosperity - in the fruit of your womb, the young of your livestock and the crops of your ground - in the land He swore to your forefathers to give you. The Lord will open the heavens, the storehouse of His bounty, to send rain on your land in season and to bless all the work of your hands. You will lend to many nations but will borrow from none. The Lord will make you the head and not the tail. If you pay attention to the commands of the Lord your God that I give you this day and carefully follow them, you will always be at the top, never at the bottom. Do not turn aside from any of the commands I give you today, to the right or to the left, following other gods and serving them. (Deuteronomy 28:1-14)

Sounds pretty good, doesn't it! That's not what we see, however, when we look at the world today - even the Christian world. There are two sides to every coin, though, and the other side of God's blessings is the curses that come when we choose to follow Satan's ways instead of God's. Let's go again to the book of Deuteronomy:

However, if you do not obey the Lord your God and do not carefully follow all His commands and decrees I am giving you today, all these curses will come upon you and overtake you.

You will be cursed in the city and cursed in the country.

Your basket and your kneading trough will be cursed.

The fruit of your womb will be cursed, and the crops of your land, and the calves of your herds and the lambs of your flocks.

You will be cursed when you come in and cursed when you go out.

(Deuteronomy 28:15-19)

This chapter of Deuteronomy has a whole host of other curses that occur when we choose to follow the Devil's path instead of God's, and they cover every calamity on the face of the earth. **There are only two paths in this world**: God's and the Devil's. If you're not following God's path, you're on the Devil's path by default. It's the only other road out there, and the Enemy will do everything He can to deceive you into taking his road instead of God's. Remember: his goal is to steal, kill and destroy - you must never forget this. However, learning the defense tactics the Lord has put in His Word will give you safety and rest. Let's take a look at some of the causes of our walking out from under God's protection, and the defense tactics God has given us to overcome them.

-Not knowing your Enemy. If you are still under the illusion that the Devil is a cute little red guy who sits on your shoulder trying to get you to be naughty, it's time to wake up and smell the coffee. The Devil comes for one reason - to steal, kill and destroy. His only goal is to get you down so far you can't get up, and get you into Hell before God can rescue you for Heaven. He hates people - *all people* - with a hate and an evil that is unimaginable to the human heart, and knowing and understanding this is the first key to walking in God's protection.

-Underestimating or not recognizing your sin. Sometimes, instead of looking at Jesus as our standard, we choose to look at the world. We think, "Well, *I'm* not as bad as so-and-so. I don't kill, or commit adultery. My sins are small, and everyone does them, and they don't really hurt anyone, so, I'm doing okay." This is a very dangerous train of thought. You can't knowingly walk in sin and stay on God's path. If you're doing this, you're playing on the Devil's playground, and eventually you're going to get hurt. As humans, we will not be sin-free until the time of the New Heaven and the New Earth, but we must, as the book of Hebrews tells us:

"throw off everything that hinders us and the sin that so easily entangles us, and let us run with perseverance the race marked out for us." (Hebrews 12:1).

Praise God, we have His grace to cover us, forgive us, and ensure our salvation, but His protection lies largely in our willingness to stay out of the Devil's yard, and to stay in God's house and yard, where we belong.

-Not believing that God loves you and wants you safe. God's Word is so clear, and it is just sad that so many people give God credit for the Devil's work. Let's go to the Word and get clear about the Lord's love and His plan for His people:

The thief comes not, but to steal, kill and destroy. I come that they may have life, and have it abundantly. (John 10:10)

For I know the plans I have for you, says the Lord, plans of good and not evil, to give you a future and a hope. (Jeremiah 29:11)

He who dwells in the Secret Place of the Most High shall abide under the shadow of the Almighty. I will say of the Lord, He is my refuge and my fortress, my God, in Him I do trust. Surely He will save you from the fowler's snare and from the deadly pestilence. He will cover you with His feathers, and under His wings you will find refuge; His faithfulness will be your shield and rampart. You will not fear the terror of night, nor the arrow that flies by day, nor the pestilence that stalks in the darkness, nor the plague that destroys at midday. A thousand may fall at your side, ten thousand at your right hand, but it will not come near you. You will only observe with your eyes and see the punishment of the wicked. If you make the Most High your dwelling - even the Lord, who is my refuge - then no harm will befall you nor shall any disaster come near your tent. For God will give His angels charge over you to guard you in all your ways; they will lift you up into their hands so you do not even strike your foot against a stone. You will tread upon the lion and the cobra, you will trample the great lion and the serpent. <u>Because he loves me," says the Lord, I will rescue him; I will protect him, for he acknowledges my Name. He will call upon me and I will answer him; I will be with him in trouble. I will deliver him and honor him. With long life will I satisfy him and show him my salvation."</u> (Psalm 91)

7. Protection with Prayer

<u>*"My prayer is not that you take them out of the world, but that you protect them from the evil one."*</u> (John 17:15)

I will both lie down in peace and sleep, for you alone, O Lord, make be dwell in safety. (Psalm 4:8)

My shield is God Most High, who saves the upright in heart. (Psalm 7:10)

He reached down from on high and took hold of me; he drew me out of deep waters. He rescued me from my powerful enemy, from my foes, who were too strong for me. They confronted me in the day of my disaster, but the Lord was my support. He brought me out into a spacious place, He rescued me because He delighted in me. The Lord has dealt with me according to my righteousness; according to the cleanness of my hands he has rewarded me. (Psalm 18: 16-20)

The Bible is overflowing with verses of God's love and desire to protect His people. However, when we have more faith in the Devil and his evil than we do in God and His good, or when we "credit" God for the Devil's work, we put ourselves again into the Enemy's camp. **We must get a clear understanding of this.** We are not to pretend the Devil doesn't exist, as this gives God the credit for the terrible works the Enemy does, and convinces us to accept them. Likewise, we are not to fear the Enemy, as his only power is in deceiving us that his work is God's, or that he has power. *The Devil only has the power that we choose to let him have through our misunderstanding of the Word of God.* God is a thousand, million, trillion times bigger than the Devil ever could be. Take a moment and try to get a glimpse of God's bigness and His power:

God created the heavens, the earth, and the entire universe

God created everything in the universe, and He created it from nothing!

God retains control over the universe. Yes, He gave man authority, which is why the earth is in such a mess, but He still, in His sovereignty, stands by us, waiting to deliver us when we choose to call on Him and let Him be the leader of our lives.

God, in His desire to have a real, true relationship with His people, gave us free will, and gave us dominion over the earth. He also knew that we as humans, we would mess things up and walk out of His will, so, He stands by, waiting to deliver us from every evil when we call on Him. What an awesome God we serve!!! We have a Father who is all good, and no evil, waiting to give us every good and perfect gift when we get into a position of obedience and submission to Him and choose to believe and receive His good gifts! Go, now, and thank Him for all that He has done for us and continues to do for us, and receive it gladly!

Now that you have a clearer understanding of God's will concerning the protection of people, and a clearer understanding of the root of our troubles, let's talk about the defense tactics we can use when praying for protection.

First, we must get into our hearts that *"God has given us authority over all the power of the Enemy, and nothing, by any means, shall harm us."* (Luke 10:19). If we don't understand that God has placed the Enemy under our feet, our faith won't match God's Word and promises of protection. The Devil is no one to fear. He is an imp. He is a little, worthless liar. He is nothing but contempt in God's sight and a hindrance to God's people. God has disowned him and has no mercy left for the rebellious one that tried to take His throne, and you shouldn't either. **The Devil's only power over you is given to him when you believe the lies that he tells you over God's promises in His Word for you.** Choose to believe God's Word today - the Word that tells you that you are sons and daughters of the Most High God!

Second, we must know, understand and believe God's many promises of protection in His Word. I have given you some here, and have more in the last chapter of this book. I urge you, however, to go to the Word yourself and look them up. Start with the book of Psalms. King David, who wrote most of the Psalms, had many, many reasons to fear the Enemy. People, in their jealousy, came at him from all sides trying to destroy him for the majority of his life. David fell into sins that most of us would never dare to fall into. Because God's great love for David, and because of David's faith in God, however, God delivered him and blessed him abundantly, and the book of Psalms is full of praises and promises for the deliverance and protection the Lord provides.

Third, we must *speak* God's words of protection and deliverance into our lives - in prayer and out of prayer. We must tame our tongue and train our spirits to stand firmly on God's promises of protection, knowing that if we have built our foundation (relationship with God and knowledge of His Word) on rock instead of sand that we will withstand all storms. And if you've still got that house on sand, get into the Word and rebuild the way God tells you to! Then, when the Devil attempts to harm you or those you love, send him back to the pits of hell where He belongs by claiming God's promises of protection in His Word. Plead the precious blood of Jesus Christ over your family and over all that you have and do, and bind that devil from treading over your authority and the gifts that God has given you. Stand on the promises of God, and do it daily. Make sure that the Enemy has a clear understanding that you know full well who you are in Christ Jesus and that you will not allow him to undermine the works and plans of God in your life and the lives of those you love. Use the Word of God - the sword of the Spirit - to defeat all that the Devil tries to put upon you and those you love. Pray for God's wisdom to be ingrained in the hearts of your family and those you love. Be always on guard, prepared for battle. Learn to recognize the Enemy's very first steps onto your territory, and shut him down immediately with the promises of God, before his little troubles turn into big troubles. The work of spiritual defense and offense you do in this area will be the best work you've ever had the pleasure to do. The very best way to do this is to gain faith in Christ by educating yourself with the Word of God.

8. Praying with others

Praying alone with the Lord is a wonderful experience that should always be at the top of your "to do" list. Praying with others, however, has blessings and benefits all its own. Let's go again to the Word and see what the Lord has to say about praying with others:

<u>Again, I tell you that if two of you on earth agree about anything you ask for, it will be done for you by my Father in Heaven. For where two or more are gathered, there I am also.</u> (Matthew 18:19-20)

Deuteronomy 32:30 tells us that *one can put a thousand* (of our enemies) *to flight and two can put ten thousand fleeing.*

The sheer multiplication of this verse alone should be enough to get you praying with others! Praying with others increases our effectiveness a minimum of 5 times, per person!

There are things to consider, however, when deciding whom to pray with, and when. Here are some guidelines to keep in mind:

1. **Pray with those who hold similar doctrinal beliefs**. Although this is not a hard and fast rule, and much can be accomplished in praying with those of different belief systems, prayers can also be hindered by praying with those of a different belief system - Christian or not. For example, let's say that you believe that healing by Christ is for today, and your prayer partner(s) do not. They may pray with you and say that they stand in agreement for complete and total healing, but do they really believe it? If not, this could hinder your prayer request. If they are saying "healing" with their mouths, and believing "death" or "sickness" with their faith, your requests are on shaky ground.

   As another example, let's say your belief system holds that salvation is God's will for everyone, and your prayer partner's belief system holds that God has pre-destined some for hell. There will be

8. Praying with others

disunity in how you pray for salvation here, and that will affect the power - or lack of it - that your prayers hold, because with every prayer that you pray for regarding salvation, you run the risk of that prayer request being hindered by your prayer partner who believes the opposite in his/her heart.

I don't believe you should ever say "no" if someone asks you to pray for them, or with them. Just make sure your prayers line up with God's will in the Word, and make sure that when you are offering up your prayer requests, you do it with others who know and believe the true Word of God. Save your in-depth, urgent prayers that you feel require the power of two or more for believers who know and understand the Word.

2. **Pray with those who will keep your prayer sessions confidential.** Many a Christian, myself included, have fallen into the trap of gossiping or breaking confidences they shouldn't have broken. Many times, we don't even realize what we are doing, or that the Enemy is deceiving us, when we break these confidences. We might think we are sharing out of concern for those involved in the prayer requests, or that it's good that we share so others can pray for the situation too. Prayer requests, however, should never be shared unless you have the direct permission of the person you are praying for. Trustworthiness must be at the top of the list when choosing your prayer partners.

3. **Praying with others successfully requires that we learn to be objective, and guard our mouths.** Many times as Christians when we hear of the struggles or sins of those we are very close to, fear takes over, and we have the desire to tell that person that they need to do A, B and C immediately to rid their lives of this problem or sin. Our fear-based answer, however, may not be the solution God has to solve this problem. Paul admonishes us in Ephesians, however, to *"Let no corrupt word proceed out of your mouth, but what is good for necessary edification, that it may impart grace to the hearer."* (Ephesians 4:29)

We need to be objective enough and patient enough when praying with others to step back from the situation and seek God's will before opening our mouths. God may certainly give you a Word for this person about their situation, but we need to make sure that that word is from God through our spirits, and not through our emotions or fears that the Enemy is working up in us. You can be just as objective when praying with your sibling or spouse as you can with the person you barely know from church, but you must first develop the patience and objectiveness of seeking God first. Then you will know and hear His will for the situation, and be able to *"impart grace to the hearer".*

The Word of God is very clear that we are to have fellowship with other believers, in prayer and out of prayer.

8. Praying with others

Let's look and see what Paul tells us in Acts Chapter 2 about fellowship with other believers:

And they continued steadfastly in the apostles' doctrine and fellowship, in the breaking of bread and in prayers. Then fear came upon every soul, and many wonders and signs were done through the apostles. Now all who believed were together, and had all things in common, and sold their possessions and goods, and divided them among all, as anyone had need. So continuing daily with one accord in the temple, and breaking bread from house to house, they ate their food with gladness and simplicity of heart, praising God and having favor with all the people. And the Lord added to the church daily those who were being saved. (Acts 2:42-47)

Make it a point to fellowship with other believers - in prayer and out of prayer. Praying with others accomplishes great thing! Just be sure to use God's instructions in His Word to pray with others in a way that glorifies God and gets things done.

9. Praying for Others

One of the biggest responsibilities we have as followers of Christ is to pray for one another. When God instructs us in the Bible to pray, it is given in a command form. Look at the verses below:

Is any one of you in trouble? He should pray. Is anyone happy? Let him sing songs of praise. Is any one of you sick? He should call the elders of the church to pray over him and anoint him with oil in the name of the Lord. And the prayer offered in faith will make the sick person well; the Lord will raise him up. If he has sinned, he will be forgiven. Therefore confess your sins to each other and pray for each other so that you may be healed. The prayer of a righteous man is effective and avails much. (James 5:13-16)

Be joyful always, pray continually; give thanks in (not *for*, but *in*) *all circumstances, for this is God's will for you* (not necessarily the circumstances but the giving of thanks in all things) *in Christ Jesus.* (1 Thessalonians 5:17, 18)

Then Jesus told His disciples in a parable to show them that they should always pray and not give up. (Luke 18:1)

<u>And when you pray, do not be like the hypocrites, for they love to pray standing in the synagogues and on the street corners to be seen by men.</u> (Matthew 6:5)

God expects prayer to be a regular part of our lives - a daily duty. Prayer releases God's power to help the people. Remember: God is a gentleman - He will not force His way into our lives or the lives of others. He gave us free will for a reason: so that we would be free to choose Him on our own will as the Lord and Savior of our lives. Anything else would be a dictatorship. Thus, He will not force His help into our lives, but is watching and waiting eagerly for us to invite Him in and *ask* for His help, that He may freely give it and protect us from the Evil One and his tactics. Choose today to release the power of God by praying for yourself, and for others in the world who need God's love and help in their lives. Let's talk now about some of the most effective ways to pray for others.

-Praying in agreement with God's will. Remember that God knows better than any human does His will for the lives of the people on this earth. God tells us in Jeremiah chapter 1:

<u>*Before I formed you in the womb, I knew you, before you were born I set you apart;*</u> (Jeremiah 1:5)

Therefore, it's important when praying for others to always seek God's wisdom for His will concerning those you are praying for. Most times, you can find God's will, for anyone, right in the Word. If you are praying for a particular situation, go to the Word and see what it says, and adjust your prayers accordingly. When praying according to the Word, we always use in our family the verses that apply to our particular request, putting the name of the person we are praying for in place of the pronoun in the particular verse. For example, when praying for someone's salvation, we say, quoting Ephesians 1, verse 18:

Lord, I pray also that the eyes of Rick's heart may be enlightened in order that he may know the hope to which you have called him…

Or, when praying for protection:

John who dwells in the Secret Place of the Most High shall abide under the shadow of the Almighty. John will say of the Lord: He is my refuge and my fortress; my God, in Him I do trust.

When you pray in this way, you can be certain that you are praying within God's will, because whatever instructions God gives us are meant for everyone. Just as we talked earlier, though, when praying for something that is not addressed specifically in the Bible, like a job change, a move, or for God to bring someone a spouse, in these situations we need to pray more abstractly. Pray for things such as:

-Wisdom for that person concerning the situation
-That he/she would have ears to hear God's voice and God's will
-That his or her ears would be shut to the lies of the Enemy
-That God would shut any doors He wants shut and open any doors He wants open concerning that situation.

This way, you are still praying for God's will, and not the person's or your own will. Guiding people to God's path for them should always be the main goal when praying for others.

-Praying offensively and defensively. This is very important because we need to remember that not only do we need to pray God's will into the lives of those we are praying for, but we need to thwart the attacks of the Enemy as well. Remember that in the book of Matthew, Jesus tells us that He has given us the keys to the kingdom of heaven, and whatever we bind on earth will be bound in heaven, and whatever we loose on earth will be loosed in heaven. This is where the words you speak are very, very important. Proverbs 18:21 tells us *that "death and life are in the power of the tongue, and*

9. Praying for Others

those who love it will eat its fruit". You must speak God's will for the person you are praying for, and you must use God's Word to stop the plans of the Enemy for that person by using your sword - the Word of God. Don't speak the lies of the Enemy over any situation, instead, speak the truth of the Word, which shows you God's will for your life.

For example: *I bind you, Devil, in the Name of Jesus, from my son. My God says that I have been given authority over all the power of the Enemy so I claim that authority in Jesus' Name and bind you from my son. I thank you, Father, that as the Word says, he will "come to a knowledge of the truth and be saved". I thank You that he will "believe and be baptized and therefore will be saved". I thank You that he will have "ears to hear" and understand the Lord's Word and the Lord's truth.*

Since, many times, the people that we are praying for can be unaware or unbelieving of the tactics the Devil is using to deceive them, we must pray for the veil of deception to be removed from their eyes. We must pray that they would know the truth and that the truth would set them free. When they are not willing to believe what a person tells them about their captivity, we must pray that God will work from the inside out - that they will learn through the gaining of Godly wisdom, and be able to see clearly the situation they are in.

Now, let me put to rest an issue that may be in your mind. You are not telling the Lord what to do here. God is sovereign, and in His grace He has given you authority over all the power of the Enemy and the creatures of the earth. You are not surpassing His sovereignty here by claiming with authority your prayer requests. You are simply standing - having faith in the Truth of God's Word, claiming what you know to be His Will for those in need of grace and mercy. This was God's purpose in adopting us as His sons and daughters, that we, like Jesus, would *"Go into all the world and preach the gospel to all creation."* (Mark 16:15). That we would go and share the good news of God's salvation to those who have been deceived by the Enemy. It is our duty and a great gift to stand in prayer, claiming God's deliverance for the captives, by praying according to His Word for those in need. Take the authority He has given you, and use it to remind the Devil that his authority has been taken from him and given back to God's people, where it belongs, and work together with the Lord, as His faithful warrior, to save the world!

-Pray without ceasing. Sometimes praying for others can be exhausting and discouraging. At times, you may pray for years for a person's salvation, deliverance or healing before seeing results. Sometimes, the answers never come. But God, remember, calls us to "pray without ceasing." There are many forces at work behind the scenes that we cannot always see or understand with our spiritual eyes. Two things will help here, in any prayer situation.

The first is to pray without ceasing. This must be done not in a way that is harassing and badgering the Lord, but in a way where you are choosing, daily, to give this situation over to Him for His guidance, power, authority and wisdom. Where we may sometimes fail and pray incorrectly, the Lord never fails, and He will, in His great mercy, guide us through the dark paths and into the light where we can see, and thus learn, to pray correctly if our hearts truly have Him as first place in our lives.

The second piece of advice that has been crucial to the success we've seen in regards to answered prayer in our family has been to seek the Lord for wisdom. When you have prayed and not heard His voice or seen an answer, ask Him for wisdom regarding the situation. Just go to Him! Say "Lord, I've done all that I know how to do, and I still am not hearing your voice or getting an answer. Please fill me with wisdom regarding this situation so that I can hear clearly your will here. I want to do what you would do, Lord, so please show me Your way." You'd be surprised how quickly roadblocks can be broken down when adding this simple request to an unanswered prayer or to a situation in which you can't discern God's will for others, or for yourself. You'll suddenly see the situation with a whole new set of eyes. You'll be able to see things with God's eyes, instead of your own, and therefore be able to apply God's wisdom and instruction in order to break down the barriers that have gotten in the way.

Praying for others is one of the greatest gifts God has given us. It is a way In which we can share the love of Christ powerfully and effectively, even if the person(s) we are praying for have no idea we're praying or don't want to know about the love of Jesus. Make a commitment today to lift up in prayer those around you, that the love of Christ may be shed abroad in your heart and in theirs!

10. Verses to Pray With

I sincerely hope that what you've read on these pages has helped you to gain a better understanding of God's Word and His will for your life. As God has directed me, I've written this last chapter to be a guide to verses that will help you to pray His will over situations in your lives. Read them and claim them for you, your family, and all those you pray for, remembering to speak only what God says in His Word about your situation. Then praise God with your whole heart, pray without ceasing and watch wonderful things happen in your lives and the lives of those you pray for as God releases His Mighty Power! May God bless you and keep you as you begin on this new journey of prayer!

Verses of praise for the Lord

I will give thanks to the Lord because of His righteousness and will sing praise to the Name of the Lord Most High. (Psalm 7:17)

From the lips of children and infants you have ordained praise because of your enemies, to silence the foe and the avenger. (Psalm 8:2)

I will praise you, O Lord, with all my heart; I will tell of all your wonders. I will be glad and rejoice in you; I will sing praise to Your Name, O Most High. (Psalm 9:1-2)

The Lord lives! Blessed by my Rock! Let the God of my salvation be exalted! (Psalm 18:46)

Enter into His gates with thanksgiving and into His courts with praise. Be thankful to Him and bless His name. For the Lord is good; His mercy is everlasting and His truth endures to all generations. (Psalm 100:4-5)

Shout for joy to the Lord, all the earth. Worship the Lord with gladness; come before Him with joyful songs. (Psalm 100:1-2)

Exalt the Lord our God and worship at His footstool; He is holy. (Psalm 99:5)

It is good to praise the Lord and make music to your name, O Most High, to proclaim your love in the morning and your faithfulness at night, (Psalm 92:1-2)

10. Verses to Pray With

The Lord is my strength and my song, and He has become my salvation; He is my God, and I will praise Him. (Exodus 15:2)

The Lord lives! Blessed be my Rock! Let God be exalted, The Rock of my salvation! (2 Samuel 22:47)

Therefore by Him let us continually offer the sacrifice of praise to God, that is, the fruit of our lips, giving thanks to His name. (Hebrews 13:15)

Is anyone happy? Let him sing songs of praise. (James 5:13)

I will give you thanks in the great assembly; among throngs of people I will praise you. (Psalm 35:18)

My tongue will speak of your righteousness and of your praises all day long. (Psalm 35:28)

Verses regarding God's safety and protection

I will both lie down in peace and sleep, for you alone, O Lord, make me dwell in safety. (Psalm 4:8)

But let all who take refuge in You be glad; let them ever sing for joy. Spread you protection over them, that those who love Your Name may rejoice in You. For surely, O Lord, you bless the righteous; you surround them with your favor as a shield. (Psalm 5:11-12)

My shield is God Most High, who saves the upright in heart. (Psalm 7:10)

I will call upon the Lord, who is worthy to be praised; so shall I be saved from my enemies. (Psalm 18:3)

<u>*Have I not commanded you? Be strong and courageous. Do not be afraid or discouraged, for the Lord your God is with you wherever you go*</u>. (Joshua 1:9)

<u>*Do not fear, for I am with you; be not dismayed, for I am your God. I will strengthen you, yes, I will help you; I will uphold you with my righteous right hand*</u>. (Isaiah 41:10)

He who dwells in the Secret Place of the Most High shall abide under the shadow of the Almighty. I will say of the Lord, "He is my refuge and my fortress, in Him I do trust. Surely God will save you from the fowler's snare and from the deadly pestilence. He will cover you with His feathers and under His wings you shall find refuge. His faithfulness will be your shield and rampart. You will not fear the terror of night, nor the arrow that flies by day, nor the pestilence that stalks in the darkness, nor the plague that destroys at midday. A thousand may fall at your side, ten thousand at your right hand, but it shall not come near you. You will only observe with your eyes and see the punishment of the wicked. Because you have made the Lord, who is your refuge, even the Most High, your dwelling place, no evil shall befall you nor shall any plague come near your dwelling. For God will give His angels charge over you to guard you in all your ways. They will lift you up into their hands so you do not even strike your foot against a stone. You will tread upon the lion and the cobra; you will trample the great lion and the serpent. <u>*"Because he loves me,"*</u> *says the Lord, "*<u>*I will rescue him; I will protect him, for he acknowledges my name. He will call upon me, and I will answer him;*</u>

10. Verses to Pray With

<u>I will be with him in trouble. I will deliver him and honor him. With long life will I satisfy him and show him my salvation.</u>" (Psalm 91)

He reached down from on high and took hold of me; he drew me out of deep waters. He rescued me from my powerful enemy, from my foes who were too strong for me. They confronted me in the day of my disaster, but the Lord was my support. He brought me out into a spacious place; he rescued me because he delighted in me. (Psalm 18:16-19)

The Lord is my shepherd, I shall not be in want. He makes me lie down in green pastures, he leads me beside still waters, he restores my soul. He guides me in paths of righteousness for his name's sake. Even though I walk through the valley of the shadow of death, I will fear no evil, for you are with me; your rod and your staff, they comfort me. You prepare a table before me in the presence of my enemies. You anoint my head with oil; my cup overflows. Surely goodness and love will follow me all the days of my life, and I will dwell in the house of the Lord forever. (Psalm 23)

The righteous cry out, and the Lord hears them; he delivers them from all their troubles. (Psalm 34:17)

The angel of the Lord encamps around those who fear Him, and he delivers them. (Psalm 34:7)

Verses regarding God's healing

When Jesus came down from the mountainside, large crowds followed Him. A man with leprosy came and knelt before Him *and said, "Lord, if you are willing, you can make me clean." Jesus reached out His hand and touched the man. "<u>I am willing</u>," he said. "<u>Be clean!</u>" Immediately the man was cured of his leprosy.* (Matthew 8:1-3)

When Jesus had entered Capernaum, a centurion came to Him, asking for help. "Lord," he said, "My servant lies at home paralyzed and in terrible suffering." Jesus said to him, "<u>I will go and heal him</u>." The centurion replied, "Lord, I do not deserve to have you come under my roof. But just say the word, and my servant will be healed. For I myself am a man under authority, with soldiers under me. I tell this one, 'Go,' and he goes; and that one, 'Come,' and he comes. I say to my servant, 'Do this,' and he does it. When Jesus heard this he was astonished and said to those following Him, "<u>I tell you the truth, I have not found anyone in Israel with such great faith. I say to you that many will come from the east and the west, and will take their places at the feast with Abraham, Isaac and Jacob in the kingdom of heaven. But the subjects of the kingdom will be thrown outside, into the darkness, where there will be weeping and gnashing of teeth</u>." Then Jesus said to the centurion, "<u>Go. It will be done just as you believed it would</u>." And his servant was healed at that very hour. (Matthew 8:5-13)

But He was wounded for our transgressions, He was bruised for our iniquities; the chastisement for our peace was upon Him, and by His stripes we are healed. (Isaiah 53:5)

But to you who fear My name the Sun of Righteousness shall arise for you with healing in His wings. (Malachi 4:2)

10. Verses to Pray With

When Jesus departed from there, two blind men followed Him, crying out and saying, "Son of David, have mercy on us!" And when He had come into the house, the blind men came to Him. And Jesus said to them, "<u>Do you believe that I am able to do this?</u>" They said to Him, "Yes, Lord." Then He touched their eyes, saying, "<u>According to your faith it will be done to you.</u>" And their eyes were opened. (Matthew 9:27-30a)

Now when Jesus had come into Peter's house, He saw his wife's mother lying sick with a fever. So He touched her hand, and the fever left her. And she arose and served them. When evening had come, they brought to Him many who were demon-possessed. And He cast out the spirits with a word, and healed all who were sick. (Matthew 8:14-16)

While He spoke these things to them, behold, a ruler came and worshiped Him, saying, "My daughter has just died, but come and lay Your hand on her and she will live."" So Jesus arose and followed him, and so did His disciples. And suddenly, a woman who had a flow of blood for twelve years came from behind and touched the hem of His garment. For she said to herself, "If only I may touch His garment, I shall be made well." But Jesus turned around, and when He saw her He said, "Be of good cheer, daughter; your faith has made you well." And the woman was made well from that hour. When Jesus came into the ruler's house and saw the flute players and the noisy crowd wailing, He said to them, "Make room, for the girl is not dead, but sleeping." And they ridiculed Him. But when the crowd was put outside, He went in and took her by the hand, and the girl arose. (Matthew 9:18-25)

Praise the Lord, O my soul, and forget not all His benefits; who forgives all your sins and heals all your diseases. (Psalm 103:2-3)

When Jesus and His disciples had crossed over, they landed at Gennesaret. And when the men of that place recognized Jesus, they sent word to all the surrounding country. People brought all their sick to Him and begged Him to let the sick just touch the edge of His cloak, and all who touched Him were healed. (Matthew 14:34-36).

And when He came near the gate of the city, behold, a dead man was being carried out, the only son of his mother; and she was a widow. And a large crowd from the city was with her. When the Lord saw her, He had compassion on her and said to her, "Do not weep." Then He came and touched the open coffin, and those who carried him stood still. And He said, "Young man, I say to you, arise." So he who was dead sat up and began to speak. And He presented him to his mother. (Luke 7:12-15)

In Lystra, there sat a man crippled in his feet, who was lame from birth and had never walked. He listened to Paul as he was speaking. Paul looked directly at him, saw that he had faith to be healed and called out, "Stand up on your feet!" At that, the man jumped up and began to walk. (Acts 14:8-10).

Is any one of you sick? He should call the elders of the church to pray over him and anoint him with oil in the name of the Lord. And the prayer offered up in faith will make the sick person well. Therefore confess your sins to each other and pray for each other so that you may be healed. The effective prayer of a righteous man avails much. (James 5:14-16)

God said, "<u>If you listen carefully to the voice of the Lord your God and do what is right in His sight, if you pay attention to His commands and keep all His decrees, I will not bring on you any of the diseases I brought on the Egyptians, for I am the Lord who heals you</u>. (Exodus 15:26)

Verses regarding God's authority and greatness

The Lord is my rock, my fortress and my deliverer; my God is my rock, in whom I take refuge. He is my shield and the horn of my salvation, my stronghold. (Psalm 18:2)

The Lord reigns forever; He has established His throne for judgment. He will judge the world in righteousness; he will govern the peoples with justice. The Lord is a refuge for the oppressed, a stronghold in times of trouble. (Psalm 9:7-9)

The Lord is in His holy temple; the Lord is on His heavenly throne. His eyes behold, His eyelids test the sons of men. The Lord tests the righteous, but the wicked and the one who loves violence His soul hates. On the wicked he will rain fiery coals and burning sulfur; a scorching wind will be their lot. For the Lord is righteous, He loves righteousness; His countenance beholds the upright. (Psalm 11:4-7)

You, O Lord, keep my lamp burning; my God turns my darkness into light. With your help I can advance against a troop; with my God I can scale a wall. As for God, His way is perfect; the word of the Lord is proven. He is a shield for all who trust in Him. For who is God besides the Lord? And who is the Rock except our God? (Psalm 18:28-31)

He will respond to the prayer of the destitute; He will not despise their plea. (Psalm 102:17)

The heavens declare the glory of God; and the firmament shows His handiwork. (Psalm 19:1)

The law of the Lord is perfect, converting the soul. The testimony of the Lord is sure, making wise the simple. The statutes of the Lord are right, giving joy to the heart. The commandment of the Lord is pure, enlightening the eyes. The fear of the Lord is clean, enduring forever. The judgments of the Lord are true and righteous altogether. More to be desired are they than gold, yea, than much fine gold; they are sweeter than honey, than honey from the comb. By them is your servant warned; in keeping them there is great reward. (Psalm 19:7-11)

Your mercy, O Lord, reaches to the heavens, your faithfulness to the clouds. (Psalm 36:5)

For the Lord your God is God of gods and Lord of lords, the great God, mighty and awesome, who shows no partiality and accepts no bribes. He defends the cause of the fatherless and the widow, and loves the stranger, giving him food and clothing. (Deuteronomy 10: 17-18)

Verses regarding the authority God has given us

What is man that you are mindful of him, the son of man that you visit him? For You have made him a little lower than the angles and crowned him with glory and honor. You made him to have dominion over the works of your hands; you put all things under his feet. (Psalm 8:4-6)

It is God who arms me with strength and makes my way perfect. He makes my feet like the feet of a deer; He sets me on high places. He teaches my hands to make war, so that my arms can bend a bow of bronze. You have also given me the shield of your salvation, your right hand has held me up; your gentleness had made me great. You enlarged my path under me, so my feet did not slip. (Psalm 18:32-36)

<u>*Behold, I give you the authority to trample on serpents and scorpions and over all the power of the Enemy, and nothing shall by any means hurt you.*</u> (Luke 10:19)

<u>*I will give you the keys of the kingdom of heaven, and whatever you bind on earth will be bound in heaven, and whatever you loose on earth will be loosed in heaven.*</u> (Matthew 16:19)

Then God said <u>*"Let us* (the Trinity) *make man in our image, according to our likeness, and let them have dominion over the fish of the sea, over the birds of the air, over the cattle, over all the earth, and over every creeping thing that creeps in the earth."*</u> (Genesis 1: 26)

But when the fullness of the time had come, God sent forth His Son, born of a woman, born under law, to redeem those who were under the law, that we might receive the adoption as sons. And because you are sons, God has sent forth the Spirit of His Son into your hearts, crying out, <u>*"Abba, Father."*</u>

Therefore you are no longer a slave, but a son; and if you are a son, then an heir of God through Christ. (Galatians 4:4-7)

The Spirit himself bears witness with our spirit that we are children of God, and if children, then heirs – heirs of God and joint heirs with Christ, if indeed we suffer with Him, that we may also be glorified together. (Romans 8:16-17)

Verses regarding God's salvation

The Lord redeems the soul of His servants; and none of those who trust in Him shall be condemned. (Psalm 34:22)

The salvation of the righteous is from the Lord; He is their strength in time of trouble. (Psalm 37:39)

Godly sorrow brings repentance leading to salvation, not to be regretted; but the sorrow of the world produces death. (2 Corinthians 7:10)

Let it be known to you all, and to all the people of Israel, that by the name of Jesus Christ of Nazareth, whom you crucified, whom God raised from the dead, by Him this man stands before you whole. This is the 'stone which was rejected by you builders, which has become the chief cornerstone'. Nor is there salvation in any other, for there is no other name under heaven given among men by which we must be saved. (Acts 4:10-12)

Rejoice greatly, O Daughter of Zion! Shout, Daughter of Jerusalem! See, your king comes to you, righteous and having

10. Verses to Pray With

salvation, gentle and riding on a donkey, on a colt, the foal of a donkey. (Zechariah 9:9)

Salvation comes from the Lord. (Jonah 2:9)

And everyone who calls on the name of the Lord will be saved. (Joel 2:32)

<u>*He who believes and is baptized will be saved.*</u> (Mark 16:16)

<u>*I am the door. If anyone enters by Me he will be saved, and will go in and out and find pasture.*</u> (John 10:9)

O Lord, you brought my soul up from the grave, you have kept me alive, that I should not go down into the pit. (Psalm 30:3)

Blessed is he whose transgression is forgiven, whose sin is covered. Blessed is the man to whom the Lord does not impute iniquity and in whose spirit there is no deceit. (Psalm 32:1-2)

The Lord redeems the soul of His servants, and none of those who trust in Him shall be condemned. (Psalm 34:22)

Verses regarding God's blessings and abundance

He sent from above, He took me; He drew me out of many waters. He delivered me from my strong enemy, from those who hated me, for they were too strong for me. They confronted me in the day of my calamity, but the Lord was my support. He also brought me out into a broad place; He delivered me because He delighted in me. The Lord rewarded me according to my righteousness; according to the cleanness of my hands He has recompensed me. (Psalm 18:16-20)

"<u>For I know the plans I have for you,</u>" says the Lord, "<u>plans of good and not evil, to give you a future and a hope.</u>" (Jeremiah 29:11)

<u>The thief comes not, but to steal, kill and destroy; I come that you may have life, and have it abundantly</u>. (John 10:10)

<u>Ask and it will be given to you; seek and you will find; knock and the door will be opened to you. For everyone who asks receives; he who seeks finds; and to him who knocks, the door will be opened.</u> (Matthew 7:7-8)

<u>If you then, though you are evil, know how to give good gifts to your children, how much more will your Father in heaven give good gifts to those who ask Him!</u> (Matthew 7:11)

All these blessings will come upon you and overtake you because you obey the voice of Lord your God: Blessed shall you be in the city, and blessed shall you be in the country. Blessed shall be the fruit of your body, the produce of your ground, and the increase of your herds, the increase of your cattle and the offspring of your flocks. Blessed shall be your basket and your kneading bowl. Blessed shall you be when you come in, and blessed shall you be when you go out. (Deuteronomy 28:2-6)

Great deliverance He gives to His king, and shows mercy to His anointed, to David and his descendants forevermore. (Psalm 18:50)

10. Verses to Pray With

May the Lord answer you in the day of trouble; May the name of the God of Jacob defend you; May He send you help from the sanctuary, and strengthen you out of Zion; May He remember all your offerings and accept your burnt sacrifice. May He grant you according to your hearts' desire and fulfill all your purpose. (Psalm 20:1-4)

Honor the Lord with your possessions, and with the first fruits of all your increase; so your barns will be filled with plenty, and your vats will overflow with new wine. (Proverbs 3:9-10)

The Lord gives strength to His people; the Lord blesses His people with peace. (Psalm 29:11)

The lions may grow weak and hungry, but those who seek the Lord lack no good thing. (Psalm 34:10)

I will be glad and rejoice in Your love, for You saw my affliction and knew the anguish of my soul. You have not handed me over to the Enemy but have set my feet in a spacious place. (Psalm 31:7-8)

Oh, how great is Your goodness, which You have laid up for those who fear You, which You have prepared for those who trust in You in the presence of the sons of men! You shall hide them in the secret place of Your presence from the plots of man; You shall keep them secretly in a pavilion from the strife of tongues. (Psalm 31:19-20)

But the eyes of the Lord are on those who fear Him, on those who hope in His unfailing love, to deliver their soul from death and keep them alive in famine. (Psalm 33: 18-19)

Taste and see that the Lord is good; blessed is the man who trusts in Him. (Psalm 34:8)

The steps of a good man are ordered by the Lord, and He delights in his way. Though he fall, he shall not be utterly cast down, for the Lord upholds him with His hand. (Psalm 37:23-24)

The Lord knows the days of the upright, and their inheritance shall be forever. They shall not be ashamed in the evil time, and in the days of famine they shall be satisfied. (Psalm 37: 18-19)

Verses regarding faith

Trust in the Lord with all your heart and lean not on your own understanding; in all your ways acknowledge Him and He will direct your paths. (Proverbs 3:5-6)

Believe in the Lord your God, and you shall be established; believe His prophets, and you shall prosper. (2 Chronicles 20:20)

"<u>I tell you the truth, if you have faith as small as a mustard seed, you can say to this mountain, 'Move from here to there' and it will move. Nothing will be impossible for you</u>." (Matthew 17:20)

"So Jesus answered and said to them, <u>"Have faith in God. For assuredly I say to you, whoever says to this mountain, 'Be removed and be cast into the sea,' and does not doubt in</u>

his heart, but believes that those things he says will be done, he will have whatever he says." (Mark 11:22-23)

For by grace you have been saved through faith, and that not of yourselves; it is the gift of God, not of works, lest anyone should boast. (Ephesians 2:8-9)

Above all, take the shield of faith, with which you will be able to quench all the fiery darts of the wicked one. (Ephesians 6:16)

Fight the good fight of faith. Take hold of the eternal life to which you were called when you made your good confession in the presence of many witnesses. (1 Timothy 6:12)

Now faith is the substance of things hoped for, the evidence of things not seen. (Hebrews 11:1)

But without faith, it is impossible to please God, for he who comes to God must believe that He is, and that He is a rewarder of those who diligently seek Him. (Hebrews 11:6)

For whatever is born of God overcomes the world. And this is the victory that has overcome the world - our faith. Who is he who overcomes the world, but he who believes that Jesus is the Son of God. (1 John 5:4-5)

Verses regarding wisdom, discernment and knowledge

But whoever listens to me will dwell safely, and will be secure, without fear of evil. (Proverbs 1:33)

My son, if you receive my words and treasure my commands within you, so that you incline your ear to wisdom, and apply your heart to understanding; yes, if you cry out for discernment and lift up your voice for understanding, if you seek her as silver, and search for her as for hidden treasures; then you will understand the fear of the Lord and find the knowledge of God. (Proverbs 2:1-5)

Do not be wise in your own eyes; fear the Lord and shun evil. This will bring health to your body and strength to your bones. (Proverbs 3:7-8)

Happy is the man who finds wisdom, and the man who gains understanding; for her proceeds are better than the profits of silver, and her gain than fine gold. She is more precious than rubies, and all the things you may desire cannot compare with her. Length of days is in her right hand, and in her left hand riches and honor. Her ways are ways of pleasantness, and all her paths are peace. She is a tree of life to those who take hold of her, and happy are all who retain her. (Proverbs 3:13-18)

Wisdom is the principal thing; therefore get wisdom. And in all your getting, get understanding. Exalt her, and she will promote you; she will bring you honor, when you embrace her. She will place on your head an ornament of grace; a crown of glory she will deliver to you. (Proverbs 4:7-9)

The fear of the Lord is the beginning of knowledge, but fools despise wisdom and instruction. (Proverbs 1:7)

10. Verses to Pray With

When wisdom enters your heart, and knowledge is pleasant to your soul, discretion will preserve you; understanding will keep you, to deliver you from the way of evil, from the man who speaks perverse things, from those who leave the paths of uprightness to walk in the ways of darkness; who rejoice in doing evil, and delight in the perversity of the wicked; whose ways are crooked, and who are devious in their paths. (Proverbs 2:12-15)

My son, preserve sound judgment and discernment, do not let them out of your sight; they will be life for you, an ornament to grace your neck. Then you will go on your way in safety, and your foot will not stumble; when you lie down, you will not be afraid; when you lie down, your sleep will be sweet. Have no fear of sudden disaster or of the ruin that overtakes the wicked, for the Lord will be your confidence and will keep your foot from being snared. (Proverbs 3:21-26)

Get wisdom, get understanding; do not forget my words or swerve from them. Do not forsake wisdom, and she will protect you; love her, and she will watch over you. (Proverbs 4:5-6)

Listen, my son, accept what I say, and the years of your life will be many. I have taught you in the way of wisdom and led you along straight paths. When you walk, your steps will not be hampered; when you run, you will not stumble. Take firm hold of instruction, do not let go; keep her, for she is your life. (Proverbs 4:10-13)

The fear of the Lord is the beginning of wisdom, and knowledge of the Holy One is understanding. (Proverbs 9:10)

Does not wisdom cry out? Does not understanding raise her voice? She takes her stand on the top of the high hill, beside the way, where the paths meet. She cries out by the gates, at the entry of the city, at the entrances of the doors: "To you, O men, I call, and my voice is to the sons of men. O you simple ones, understand prudence, and you fools, be of an understanding hearts. Listen, for I will speak of excellent things, and from the opening of my lips will come right things; for my mouth will speak truth; wickedness is an abomination to my lips. All the words of my mouth are with righteousness; nothing crooked or perverse is in them. They are all plain to him who understands, and right to those who find knowledge. Receive my instruction, and not silver, and knowledge rather than choice gold; for wisdom is better than rubies, and all the things one may desire cannot be compared with her. I, wisdom, dwell with prudence, and find out knowledge and discretion. The fear of the Lord is to hate evil; pride and arrogance and the evil way and the perverse mouth I hate. Counsel is mine, and sound wisdom; I am understanding, I have strength. By me kings reign, and rulers decree justice. By me princes rule, and nobles, and all the judges of the earth. I love those who love me, and those who seek me diligently will find me. Riches and honor are with me, enduring riches and righteousness. My fruit is better than gold, yes, than find gold, and my revenue than choice silver. I traverse the way of righteousness, in the midst of the paths of justice, that I may cause those who love me to inherit wealth, that I may fill their treasuries. (Proverbs 8:1-21)

10. Verses to Pray With

Verses regarding God's love and compassion for us

In your unfailing love you have led forth the people you have redeemed. (Exodus 15:13)

Many are the woes of the wicked, but the Lord's unfailing love surrounds the man who trusts in Him. (Psalm 32:10)

But the eyes of the Lord are on those who fear Him, on those whose hope is in His unfailing love. (Psalm 33:18).

Your love, O Lord, reaches to the heavens, your faithfulness to the skies. (Psalm 36:5)

How precious is Your lovingkindness, O God. Therefore the children of men put their trust under the shadow of Your wings. (Psalm 36:7)

Delight yourself also in the Lord, and He shall give you the desires of your heart. (Psalm 37:4)

Praise be to God, who has not rejected my prayer or withheld His love from me. (Psalm 66:20)

For the Lord is good and His love endures forever; His truth continues through all generations. (Psalm 100:5)

The Lord is compassionate and gracious, slow to anger, abounding in love. (Psalm 103:8)

For as high as the heavens are above the earth, so great is His love for those who fear Him; (Psalm 103:11)

For great is Your love, higher than the heavens; your truth reaches to the skies. (Psalm 108:4)

For great is His love toward us, and the faithfulness of the Lord endures forever. (Psalm 117:2)

O Israel, put your hope in the Lord, for with the Lord is unfailing love and with Him is full redemption. (Psalm 130:7)

I have loved you with an everlasting love: I have drawn you with lovingkindness. (Jeremiah 31:3)

Because of the Lord's great love we are not consumed, for His compassions never fail. They are new every morning; great is your faithfulness. (Lamentations 3:22-23)

But God demonstrates His own love for us in this; while we were still sinners, Christ died for us. (Romans 5:8)

Who shall separate us from the love of Christ? Shall trouble or hardship or persecution or famine or nakedness or danger or sword? As it is written: "For your sake we are killed all day long; we are considered as sheep to be slaughtered." No, in all these things we are more than conquerors through Him who loved us. For I am convinced that neither death nor life, nor angels nor principalities nor powers, neither the present nor the future, neither height nor depth, nor anything other created thing, will be able to separate us from the love of God that is in Christ Jesus our Lord. (Romans 8:35-39)

10. Verses to Pray With

Verses regarding forgiveness, mercy and grace

For the Lord your God is a merciful God; He will not forsake or destroy you or forget the covenant with your forefathers, which He swore to them. (Deuteronomy 4:31)

In His love and mercy He redeemed them; He lifted them up and carried them all the days of old. (Isaiah 63:9)

Praise be to the God and Father of our Lord Jesus Christ. In His great mercy he has given us new birth into a living hope through the resurrection of Jesus Christ from the dead… (1 Peter 1:3)

If you, O Lord, kept a record of sins, O Lord, who could stand? But with you there is forgiveness; therefore you are feared. (Psalm 130:3-4)

O Lord, do not rebuke me in your anger or discipline me in your wrath. Be merciful to me, Lord, for I am faint; O Lord, heal me, for my bones are in agony. My soul is in anguish. How long, O Lord, how long? Turn, O Lord, and deliver me; save me because of your unfailing love. (Psalm 6:1-4)

The Lord has heard my cry for mercy; the Lord accepts my prayer. All my enemies will be ashamed and dismayed; they will turn back in sudden disgrace. (Psalm 6:8-10)

For sin shall not have dominion over you, for you are not under law, but under grace. (Romans 6:14)

But where sin increased, grace increased all the more, so that, just as sin reigned in death, so also grace might reign through righteousness to bring eternal life through Jesus Christ our Lord. (Romans 5:20-21)

For you know the grace of our Lord Jesus Christ, that though He was rich, yet for your sakes He became poor, so that you through His poverty might become rich. (2 Corinthians 8:9)

And God is able to make all grace abound to you, that you, always having all sufficiency in all things, may have an abundance for every good work. (2 Corinthians 9:8)

And He said to me, <u>"My grace is sufficient for you, for my power is made perfect in weakness."</u> (2 Corinthians 12:9)

In Him we have redemption through His blood, the forgiveness of sins, according to the riches of His grace which He made to abound toward us in all wisdom and prudence. (Ephesians 1:7-8)

For it is by grace you have been saved, through faith - and this not from yourselves, it is the gift of God- (Ephesians 2:8)

For the grace of God that brings salvation has appeared to all men, teaching us that, denying ungodliness and worldly lusts, we should live soberly, righteously, and godly in the present age, looking for the blessed hope and glorious appearing of our great God and Savior Jesus Christ, who gave Himself for us, that He might redeem us from every lawless deed and purify for Himself His own special people, zealous for good works. (Titus 2:11-14)

10. Verses to Pray With

Verses regarding obedience

Blessed is the man who walks not in the counsel of the ungodly, nor stands in the path of sinners, nor sits in the seat of the scornful; but his delight is in the law of the Lord, and in His law he meditates day and night. He shall be like a tree planted by the rivers of water, that brings forth its fruit in its season, whose leaf also shall not wither; and whatever he does shall prosper. (Psalm 1:1-3)

Lead me, O Lord, in your righteousness because of my enemies - make straight your way before me. (Psalm 5:8)

I will walk in my house with a blameless heart. I will set nothing wicked before my eyes. (Psalm 101:2b-3a)

The Lord has rewarded me according to my righteousness, according to the cleanness of my hands in his sight. (Psalm 18:24)

May the words of my mouth and the meditation of my heart be pleasing in your sight, O Lord, my strength and my Redeemer. (Psalm 19:14)

Some trust in chariots and some in horses, but we trust in the name of the Lord our God. (Psalm 20:7)

My son, hear the instruction of your father, and do not forsake the law of your mothers; for they will be a graceful ornament on your head, and chains about your neck. (Proverbs 1:8-9)

My son, do not forget my law, but let your heart keep my commands; for length of days and long life and peace they will add to you. (Proverbs 3:1-2)

The curse of the Lord is on the house of the wicked, but He blesses the home of the righteous. (Proverbs 3:33)

The path of the righteous is like the first gleam of dawn, shining every brighter till the full light of day. (Proverbs 4:18)

My son, give attention to my words; incline your ear to my sayings. Do not let them depart from your eyes; keep them in the midst of your heart; for they are life to those who find them, and health to all their flesh. Keep your heart with all diligence, for out of it spring the issues of life. Put away from you a deceitful mouth and put perverse lips far from you. Let your eyes look straight ahead, and your eyelids look right before you. Ponder the path of your feet and let all your ways be established. Do not turn to the right or to the left; remove your foot from evil. (Proverbs 4:20-27)

Let not mercy and truth forsake you, bind them around your neck, write them on the tablet of your heart, and so find favor and high esteem in the sight of God and man. (Proverbs 3:3-4)

Fear the Lord, you His saints, for those who fear Him lack nothing. (Psalm 34:9)

The days of the blameless are known to the Lord, and their inheritance will endure forever. They shall not be ashamed in the evil time, and in the days of famine they shall be satisfied. (Psalm 37:18-19)

Verses regarding patience and perseverance

May our Lord Jesus Christ Himself and God our Father, who loved us and by His grace gave us eternal encouragement and good hope, encourage your hearts and establish you in every good word and work. (2 Thessalonians 2:16)

But the fruit of the Spirit is love, joy, peace, patience, kindness, goodness, faithfulness, gentleness and self-control. (Galatians 5:22)

For this reason we also, since the day we heard it, do not cease to pray for you, and to ask that you may be filled with the knowledge of His will in all wisdom and spiritual understanding; that you may walk worthy of the Lord, fully pleasing Him, being fruitful in every good work and increasing in the knowledge of God; strengthened with all might, according to His glorious power, for all patience and longsuffering with joy; giving thanks to the Father who has qualified us to be partakers of the inheritance of the saints in the light. (Colossians 1:9-12)

Therefore, as the elect of God, holy and beloved, put on tender mercies, kindness, humility, meekness, longsuffering; (Colossians 3:12)

A hot-tempered man stirs up dissension, but a patient man calms a quarrel. (Proverbs 15:18)

Do not be lagging in diligence, be fervent in spirit, serving the Lord; rejoicing in hope, patient in tribulations, continuing steadfastly in prayer.. (Romans 12:11-12)

Love is patient, love is kind. It does not envy, it does not boast, it is not proud. (1 Corinthians 13:4)

I therefore, the prisoner of the Lord, beseech you to walk worthy of the calling with which you were called, with all lowliness and gentleness, with longsuffering, bearing with one another in love. (Ephesians 4:1-2)

Now we exhort you, brethren, warn those who are unruly, comfort the fainthearted, uphold the weak, be patient with all. (1 Thessalonians 5:14)

I waited patiently for the Lord; and He inclined to me, and heard my cry. (Psalm 40:1)

But hope that is seen is no hope at all. Who hopes for what he already has? But if we hope for what we do not yet have, we eagerly wait for it with perseverance. (Romans 8:24b-25)

Therefore, having been justified by faith, we have peace with God through our Lord Jesus Christ, through whom also we have access by faith, into this grace in which we stand, and rejoice in hope of the glory of God. And not only that, but we also glory in tribulations, knowing that tribulation produces perseverance; and perseverance, character; and character, hope. Now hope does not disappoint, because the love of God has been poured out in our hearts by the Holy Spirit who was given to us. (Romans 5:1-5)

10. Verses to Pray With

Therefore we also, since we are surrounded by so great a cloud of witnesses, let us lay aside every weight, and the sin which so easily ensnares us, and let us run with endurance the race that is set before us… (Hebrews 12:1)

My brethren, count it all joy when you fall into various trials, knowing that the testing of your faith produces patience. But let patience have its perfect work, that you may be perfect and complete, lacking nothing. (James 1:2-4)

But also for this very reason, giving all diligence, add to your faith virtue, to virtue knowledge, to knowledge self-control, to self-control perseverance, to perseverance godliness, to godliness brotherly kindness and to brotherly kindness love. (2 Peter 1:5-7)

Take heed to yourself and your doctrine. Continue in them, for in doing this you will save both yourself and those who hear you. (1 Timothy 4:16)

Therefore do not cast away your confidence, which has great reward. For you have need of endurance, so that after you have done the will of God, you may receive the promise. (Hebrews 10:35-36)

Indeed we count them blessed who endure. You have heard of the perseverance of Job and seen the end intended by the Lord - that the Lord is very compassionate and merciful. (James 5:11)

Blessed is the man who endures temptation; for when he has been approved, he will receive the crown of life which the Lord has promised to those who love Him. (James 1:12)

Love does not rejoice in iniquity, but rejoices in the truth. Love bears all things, believes all things, hopes all things, endures all things. (Corinthians 13:6-7)

Verses regarding deliverance

Lord, how they have increased who trouble me! Many are they who rise up against me. Many are they who say of me, "There is no help for him in God." But You, O Lord, are a shield for me, my glory and the One who lifts up my head. I cried to the Lord with my voice and He heard me from His holy hill. I lay down and slept; I awoke, for the Lord sustained me. I will not be afraid of ten thousands of people who have set themselves against me all around. Arise, O Lord; save me, O my God! For you have struck all my enemies on the cheekbone; you have broken the teeth of the ungoldly. Salvation belongs to the Lord, Your blessing is upon Your people. (Psalm 3)

O, let the wickedness of the wicked come to an end, but establish the just; for the righteous God tests the hearts and minds, my defense is of God, who saves the upright in heart. (Psalm 7:9-10)

Those who know your name will trust in you, for you, Lord, have never forsaken those who seek you. (Psalm 9:10)

When my enemies turn back, they shall fall and perish at Your presence. For You have maintained my right and my cause; You sat on the throne judging in righteousness. (Psalm 9:3-4)

The righteous cry out, and the Lord hears them; He delivers them from all their troubles. (Psalm 34:17)

10. Verses to Pray With

A righteous man may have many troubles, but the Lord delivers him from them all; he protects all his bones, not one of them will be broken. (Psalm 34: 19-20)

The Lord helps the righteous and delivers them; He delivers them from the wicked and saves them, because they trust in Him. (Psalm 37:40)

For great is your mercy toward me; you have delivered me from the depths of Sheol. (Psalm 86:13)

If I say, "My foot slips," Your mercy, O Lord, will hold me up. (Psalm 94:18)

Blessed is he who considers the poor; the Lord will deliver him in time of trouble. (Psalm 41:1)

For the Lord will judge His people and He will have compassion on His servants. (Psalm 135:14)

For He will deliver the needy when he cries, the poor also, and him who has no helper. (Psalm 72:12)

Yes, we had the sentence of death in ourselves, that we should not trust in ourselves but in God who raises the dead, who delivered us from so great a death, and does deliver us; in whom we trust that He will still deliver us, (2 Corinthians 1: 9-10)

You are my hiding place; You shall preserve me from trouble; You shall surround me with songs of deliverance. (Psalm 32:7)

Use these verses as your blessed promises from God, and stand in faith as you go before the throne of grace. God bless you!

About the Author

Laurie Blank is a freelance writer and editor, and Moving Mountains is her first completed book writing. She and her husband live in Minnesota and are homeschooling parents to their four children. Her professional career has also included almost two decades in banking and mortgage, along with business ownership, administration and management. Her family being her greatest love, second only to God, she now makes her primary career out of improving her skills as a wife and mother, doing freelance writing and teaching in the areas of Christian philosophy, personal finance and financial independence, and also spends her time serving in several different ministry capacities.

Made in the USA
San Bernardino, CA
08 November 2015